Walt Disney's

MAGIC KINGDOM

Disneyland U.S.A.

ANAHEIM, CALIFORNIA

To all who come to this happy place…
WELCOME.

Disneyland is your land. Here age relives fond memories
of the past…and here youth may savor the challenge and
promise of the future.

Disneyland is dedicated to the ideals, the dreams, and the
hard facts that have created America…with the hope
that it will be a source of joy and inspiration to all the
world.

LEGEND

★ RIDES & ATTRACTIONS
◉ FUTURE DEVELOPMENTS
🅡 RESTROOMS
🅣 TELEPHONES
✚ FIRST AID
🅜 POLICE (LOST & FOUND)

WALT DISNEY'S
Disneyland

Chris Nichols

with Charlene Nichols

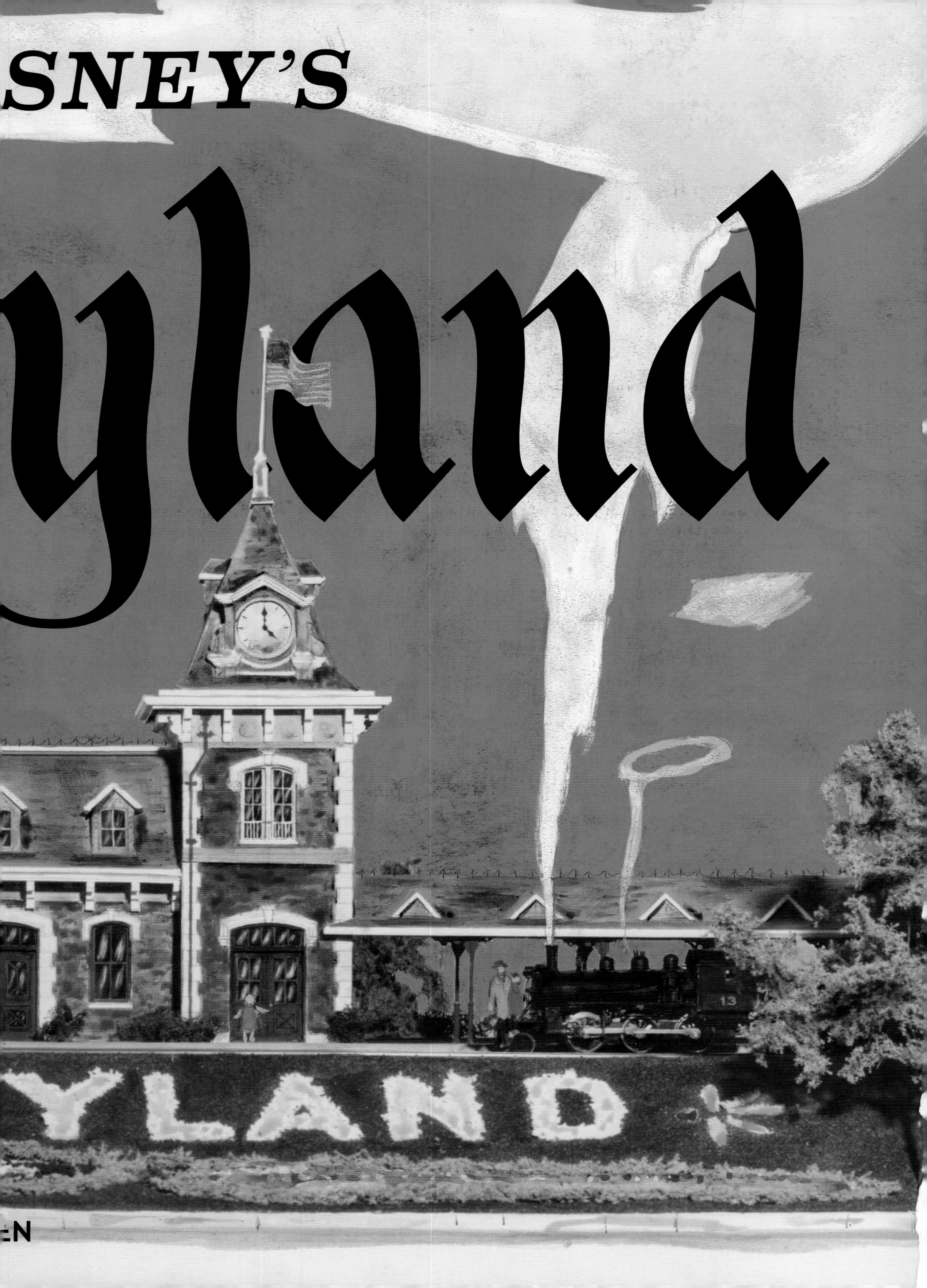
SNEY'S
yland
YLAND

Introduction

Once Upon a Time…

Sometimes Disneyland feels like it has always been here, as if it just grew out of the Earth fully formed. The park created by Walt Disney has become such an integral part of our lives, such a piece of Americana, that we forget those original 160 acres in Anaheim were once just another orange grove.

Disneyland, as we know it, could only have happened in the time and place that it did. During the mid-1950s, America was in the midst of a baby boom, Southern California was an ideal climate for a year-round outdoor attraction, and Los Angeles was teeming with movie artists and engineers who were building new lives in a postwar suburban utopia. More importantly, it was the place Walt Disney, the world's most famous film and animation producer, called home.

Although many have tried, no park has had the lasting or far-reaching impact of Disneyland. From the very beginning, its themes have been so carefully crafted that it feels like a real place — part idealized past and part conceivable future, tinged with a romanticized exoticism. "A theme park without rides is still a theme park," wrote J. G. O'Boyle in *Persistence of Vision*. "An amusement park without rides is a parking lot with popcorn."

At the dedication ceremony on opening day, July 17, 1955, Walt Disney outlined the themes of the park:

Main Street, U.S.A., was where "age relives fond memories of the past." There, the pace was slower, harkening back to

OPPOSITE **In good company — Walt Disney is joined in 1964 by some of his most adored characters. Many starred in what Walt called "classic stories of everyone's youth" that, in Fantasyland, had "become realities for youngsters of all ages to participate in."** *Photo, Lawrence Schiller*

13

Welcome to Disneyland

This is your personal map and information guide to the Happiest Place on Earth — Walt Disney's Magic Kingdom, Disneyland.

Please remember that all of us at Disneyland, your Hosts and Hostesses, always welcome the opportunity to help make your visits more pleasant and enjoyable.

Your happiness is our first consideration.

The Disneyland Staff

©Copyright, 1956, by Disneyland, Inc.

the early 1900s, before the hectic nature of the modern day, when speed limits were dictated by actual *horse*power.

Tomorrowland, on the other hand, imagined life decades away. A child could "savor the challenge and promise" of his or her own future by learning what science and technology were achieving today, and hoped to accomplish tomorrow.

Frontierland was dedicated to the "color, romance, and drama of frontier America as it developed from wilderness trails to roads, riverboats, railroads, and civilization." It captured the history of the country and was a tribute to "the ideals, the dreams, and the hard facts that have created America."

Adventureland showcased the spirit and promise of exploring uncharted territory, inspired by Disney's Academy Award–winning *True-Life Adventures* nature documentaries.

Fantasyland brought the storybook world of Disney's animated films to life as medieval-inspired pavilions from the old world — where wishing upon a star makes dreams come true.

In the chaos of the park's opening day a fair-haired boy and girl were picked out of the crowd and invited to meet Walt Disney: seven-year-old Michael Schwartner and his five-year-old cousin, Christine Vess. "I was just a kid but he talked to me like a real person," Schwartner told the *Orange County Register* during the park's 60th anniversary. "He asked me if I could wiggle my ears. I said, 'No, can you?' He said, 'Nope, but I can wiggle my nose.' And he did — mustache and all."[1] The cartoonist, studio boss, TV star, and theme-park builder took pictures and joked around with both kids, and then brought their entire families aboard his beloved railroad, and took them on a guided tour.

The combined themes of Disneyland — of nature, fantasy, exploration, and introspection, of hard work and inspiration, the past combined with the present to create the promise of the future — were similar to those of its birthplace. The park was the ultimate reflection of Southern California at mid-century, drenched in sunshine and optimism. Disneyland may be a real place, but it has revealed itself to be so much more, a statement of who we are as people, a cultural touchstone, every bit as unifying as Carl Sagan's Voyager Golden Record or Beethoven's Fifth Symphony. A place so grounded in the human spirit it becomes magic.

Walt's Dream

1901-1954

Southern California's Happiest Export

From fantasy to the future, Southern California had it all

"Saturday was always Daddy's day," Walt Disney told Canadian broadcaster Fletcher Markle of the time he spent with his daughters when they were young. "I'd take them to the merry-go-round and I took them to different places and as I'd sit…on a bench, you know, eating peanuts — I felt that there should be something built, some kind of an amusement enterprise where the parents and the children could have fun together."[1] It's the oft-repeated tale of a dreamer's first imaginings, and one that touches on a common truth. Haven't all adults wished we could play the way we did as kids again?

The storybook-like cottage Walt shared with his wife, Lillian, and their daughters, Diane and Sharon, was nestled in the Los Feliz foothills at 4053 Woking Way. It was a short walk to Los Angeles's Griffith Park, one of the largest urban parks in North America, with more than 3,000 acres of hilly ranchland and several attractions that would be mirrored in Disneyland years later.

Perched like a crown on the ridgeline's peak, Griffith Park's 1935 Art Deco observatory — filled with exhibits by leading scientists to demonstrate cutting-edge technology — could be seen as one of the earliest forerunners to Tomorrowland. Its merry-go-round helped provide inspiration for the King Arthur Carrousel at the center of Fantasyland. At the nearby Griffith Park Riding Academy, people could rent horses and ride through the park on 50 miles of bridle trails, just as visitors to early Frontierland would take horse and mule rides. The canyon known as Fern Dell contained thousands of exotic ferns dotting a natural stream with *faux bois* and stone terraces. Its pools filled with blooming water irises recall the exotic flora of Adventureland. Since 1948, kids could enjoy rides on the Griffith Park & Southern Railroad's miniature trains, and in 1952 the Travel Town museum opened, filled with various antique modes of transportation including historic locomotives, a circus car, caboose, turn-of-the-century streetcar, and horse-drawn dray wagon.

But a rural park in an urban setting was just the starting point for Walt's vision. He (and his early Imagineers) spent years researching, drawing inspiration from trips to amusements across California, the United States, and in Europe; from his childhood experiences; and from his own animated films to create the park that changed the world.

Riding the rails to a bright new tomorrow, Walt arrived in California at the age of 21, and spent most of his life there, but grew up in Illinois and Missouri. He was born in Chicago on December 5, 1901 — before man could fly or the automobile replaced the horse. From a family of modest means, he worked from a young age at a time when ships and steam locomotives were the sole modes of long-distance travel. Walt once recalled his youthful escapades on the train in Marceline, Missouri:

PREVIOUS **Walt's penchant for trains led to the construction of a miniature railroad, which was later installed in his backyard. Walt named the steam-powered locomotive "Lilly Belle" after his wife, Lillian.**

OPPOSITE **Walt Disney's world-famous Mickey Mouse was about to be joined by Walt's new venture, Disneyland. He called it "a metropolis of the future, a show place of magic and living facts," in** *Look* **magazine's November 1954 article previewing the park.** *Photo, Earl Theisen*

One day in about 1909, while I was 8 or 9 years old and full of nerve, my buddies dared me to climb into the cab of one of them that stood there, temporarily deserted, and pull the whistle cord.... As soon as the whistle shrieked I quickly climbed down in a panic and ran like the dickens.[2]

Maybe that's when he first fell in love with trains. Or maybe it was when, as a nine-year-old boy, he rode the train that circled Electric Park, an amusement park in Kansas City, to watch the nightly fireworks show. Or later at age 15, when following in brother Roy's footsteps, he spent the summer selling newspapers and snacks on the Santa Fe railroad line. There was also the train ride he took upon returning home from his post–World War I stint with the American Red Cross Ambulance Corps in France. Walt's continuing fascination with the escapism promised by rail travel would evolve from a series of ideas in studio workrooms to the acreage in Anaheim that became Disneyland. Trains — from the steam locomotives to the futuristic Monorail — would become an important feature of Disneyland, connecting the different realms to create an immersive environment.

It was during the summer of 1923 that he would board another train, this one bound for Hollywood. Two years earlier, Walt had begun his animation career in Kansas City, but he lost his first studio, Laugh-O-gram

Films, Inc., which prompted his move to California. "It was a big day the day I got on that Santa Fe Limited.... I was just free and happy," Walt remembered. "But I'd failed. And I think it's important to have a good hard failure when you're young."[3] Such experiences shaped lifelong beliefs, his ability to overcome hardship through perseverance, nostalgia for a way of life that faded away around him, and optimism about his ability to start over from scratch.

Walt set up a camera stand in his uncle's garage in Los Feliz, then a studio in the back of a realty company down the block. By 1926 Walt and Roy began building their first major movie studio together in the neighborhood of Silver Lake, where the first Mickey Mouse cartoons were created. Walt brought a sophistication to movie shorts, and in 1937 released the groundbreaking feature film *Snow White and the Seven Dwarfs*. That success enabled him to build a larger movie studio in Burbank, a luxurious moderne complex that he designed from the ground up and constructed near the Warner Bros. lot, with the help of industrial designer Kem Weber. The Burbank studio had everything he needed, and a little extra room to grow.

Around this time, Walt won a special Academy Award for *Snow White and the Seven Dwarfs* (featuring one full-size Oscar statuette surrounded by seven miniature versions), and he attended the 1939

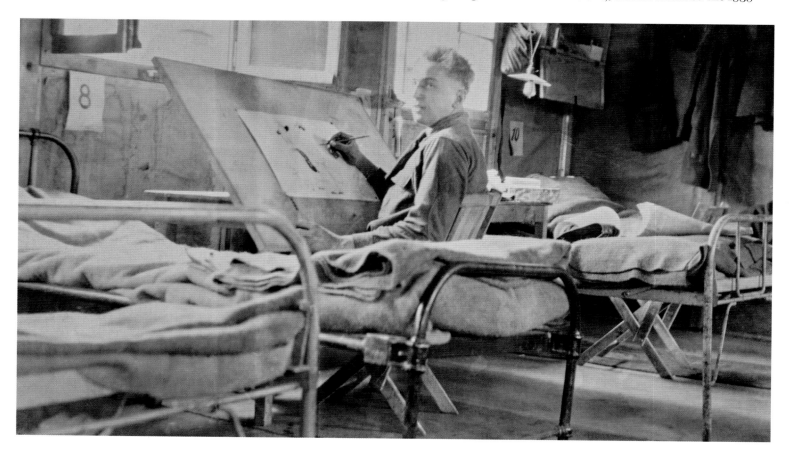

wished to have "something to show people who wanted to visit the Disney Studios."[5] One idea was a seven-acre site featuring pony rides, "singing" waterfalls, soundstage tours, a picnic space, and a scale-model passenger train.

In the summer of 1948, Walt invited studio animator and train aficionado Ward Kimball to the Chicago Railroad Fair, which honored the centennial of the first steam engine to enter that city. They traveled there (naturally by train) aboard the Super Chief from Pasadena, and were treated by the president of the Santa Fe railroad to ride up front and blow the whistle. The fairgrounds included a replica of the French Quarter in New Orleans, a dude ranch, a national park with an erupting geyser (reminiscent of scenery and show elements later featured in the early Frontierland attraction, Mine Train Through Nature's Wonderland) and the Santa Fe–sponsored Indian Village, all encircled by train tracks that could transport visitors from attraction to attraction. The themes of the exhibits were reflected in the workers' costumes and the food served, just as they later would be in Disneyland. The Railroad Fair has been largely forgotten, but it was a grand and inspiring event for both men.

From there they took a detour to the Henry Ford Museum and Greenfield Village in Dearborn, Michigan. Walt shared many of Ford's aspirations, which the automaker related to his secretary, Ernest Liebold, prior to the museum's opening:

I'm going to start up a museum and give people a true picture of the development of the country. That's the only history that is worth observing…We'll show the people what actually existed in years gone by and we'll show the actual development of American industry from the earliest days that we can recollect up to the present day.[6]

Years later Kimball would recall how "Disneyland was already forming in his mind" as Walt strolled down the "Main Street" of Greenfield Village with its 19th-century shops, early American automobiles, horse-drawn carriages, and, of course, a train. Though Walt felt his park should also have a full-size steam train "that he could have fun operating himself on days when the park was closed."[7]

Shortly after returning from Illinois, on August 31, 1948, Walt sent a memo to one of his production designers, Dick Kelsey,

ABOVE Over 30,000 fans, including nine-year-old actress Shirley Temple, descended on the Carthay Circle Theatre in Los Angeles, for the premiere of *Snow White and the Seven Dwarfs* on December 21, 1937. Surveying the miniature "Dwarfland" built across from the theater, Disney told animator Wilfred Jackson how he hoped to someday build an entire park scaled to the size of children.

OPPOSITE When he was away on business, Walt often sent telegrams to his brother Roy. One dated March 13, 1928, was sent from New York just after Walt learned they lost the rights to their popular animated character Oswald the Lucky Rabbit. Despite this, Walt wrote: "DON'T WORRY EVERYTHING OK." Indeed, it would be. On his train trip back to Los Angeles, Walt created the character that would launch the Disney empire: Mickey Mouse.

Golden Gate International Exposition in San Francisco, where he visited the Union Pacific exhibit in the Vacationland building. It featured the Civil War–era Central Pacific 173 engine that Walt would recreate in miniature for his own backyard.

Walt often entertained visitors at the studio and had big plans for his Burbank property from its start in 1939, but the outbreak of World War II stalled several of his projects, and it would take another decade for him to begin working in earnest on the concept of a family entertainment park. "We had about 30 acres (12 ha) [to build the new studio] and began to think about the land for an amusement park," Walt remembered. "Then came the war and the plans were put aside."[4]

One of the earliest accounts of Walt's plans comes from Ben Sharpsteen, codirector of the 1940 film *Fantasia*. On their trip to New York to test the new "Fantasound" speaker system, Walt told Sharpsteen he that outlined his early ideas for a village green ringed by little shops, a town hall, fire station, an opera house, restaurants, and a movie theater: "It will be a place for people to sit and rest," Walt wrote. "Mothers and grandmothers can watch over small children at play. I want it to be very relaxing, cool, and inviting." A train would connect to the live steamers at Griffith Park. Ponies evolved into a horse and carriage ride with sections added for carnival, Western, and, just as Santa Fe had done, "Indian" compounds: "I don't want to just entertain kids with pony rides and swings, I want them to learn something about their heritage."[8]

Walt sent personnel to look for an antique carousel in Europe and began researching steamboats.[9] But by October 1948, the plans had been sidelined due to his other obligations. He wrote to a Santa Fe executive he had befriended at the railroad fair: "To tell the truth, I've been so involved in production matters since I got back, that I haven't given any further thought to the project."[10]

A world in miniature

Animator Wilfred Jackson said that Walt initially broached the idea of an amusement park during the *Snow White and the Seven Dwarfs* premiere in Los Angeles on December 21, 1937. The world's first animated feature film debuted at a lavish event at the Carthay Circle Theatre in the Miracle Mile district (the facade later recreated at Disney's Hollywood Studios and Disney California Adventure Park) and included a blue carpet, klieg lights, and a live NBC radio broadcast. Walt had walkaround characters of the Seven Dwarfs available to meet guests, and an outdoor walk-through attraction called "Dwarfland," featuring a Dwarf's rustic cottage like the one seen in the film, built in the median along McCarthy Vista. More than 30,000 fans showed up at the gala to cheer the arriving stars, from Marlene Dietrich and Douglas Fairbanks Jr. to nine-year-old Shirley Temple. As they strolled by, Walt told Jackson that he wanted to build an entire park scaled to

> ### "Walt was the most enthusiastic salesman you ever met in your life. He could sell ice in the winter."
>
> **—Richard M. Sherman**

the size of children. More than 15 years of research were still ahead of him in achieving that dream.

During Walt Disney's visit to the 1939 Golden Gate International Exposition in San Francisco, he was fascinated by the Thorne Collection display of architectural miniatures, scale-model historical rooms complete with theatrical lighting and everyday objects, including little books left strewn about by an imagined reader, and a tiny cup and saucer abandoned on the edge of a table. The miniatures inspired Walt to visit contemporary recreations of historic villages over the next decade, including Henry Ford's Greenfield Village in Michigan and Colonial

Williamsburg in Virginia, where actors portrayed townsfolk living in the rebuilt 18th-century town. In 1947, he would also begin collecting miniatures from specialty shops in Europe and on the East Coast for his model train layouts.

An idea began to form, and Walt would call it Disneylandia: a traveling display of miniature Americana, a turn-of-the-20th-century village that would travel the country installed inside vintage rail cars. He gathered a team of designers and engineers who would eventually lead the creative team behind Disneyland, including Ken Anderson, Harper Goff, and Roger Broggie, and got to work. The team set to building a sample

diorama—a model of Granny Kincaid's cabin from one of the studio's live-action films that was then in production, *So Dear to My Heart* (1949). In 1952, the first "Disneylandia" display opened to the public at the Festival of California Living at the Pan-Pacific Auditorium in Los Angeles. But Walt eventually shelved the project, unhappy with the crowd dynamics, the fragility of the display, and the lack of a "wow" factor.

Looking elsewhere for ideas, Walt took his family to Madurodam, a brand-new amusement park in Holland made up entirely of 1:25 scale replicas of a Dutch city as it evolved over the centuries. At Madurodam, guests walked through the attractions, but

Willie, The Blue Whale   *Children's Fairyland, Oakland, California*

Walt would later improve on that experience (and address the issues with the Disneylandia exhibit) with the innovative Storybook Land Canal Boats attraction at Disneyland. With it, he figured out a way to tell a story, control crowds, and keep hands away from the delicate works of art.

TV personality Art Linkletter recalled a trip to Copenhagen with Walt in the summer of 1951. Tivoli Gardens, built in 1843, was the destination:

> He was making notes all the time about the lights, the chairs, the seats, and the food. I asked him what he was doing, and he replied, "I'm just making notes about something that I've always dreamed of, a great, great playground."[11]

In addition to learning about operations, maintenance, and lighting, Walt was impressed with the wandering musicians, marching bands, and live performances in the park.

Another first for California

Although Walt Disney had roots in the Midwest, sought financing on the East Coast, and visited amusements all over the globe, in the end California would be the focus of his most ambitious project to date.

His ultimate creation would take inspiration from the state that changed storytelling through the art form of film; dining through the innovations of McDonald's; urban planning through the decentralized suburban metropolis; work through computer advances at Stanford University and the University of California at Los Angeles; and even people's understanding of their place in the universe, at institutions like NASA's Jet Propulsion Laboratory and Ames Research Center.

ABOVE Walt visited Children's Fairyland in Oakland, California, soon after it opened in 1950. There, he met Willie the Whale, which could have inspired Monstro, the whale in Fantasyland. Walt later hired the park's director, Dorothy Manes, to work as youth director at Disneyland, where she would spend almost two decades.

BELOW Walt and animator Ward Kimball attended the Chicago Railroad Fair the summer it opened in 1948. The fair, which ran for two years, celebrated the centennial of Western rail and featured an Indian Village, a dude ranch, and a replica of New Orleans's French Quarter—all of which would inspire attractions at Frontierland.

Southern California in particular was a hotbed of whimsical fantasy architecture, often created by set designers-cum-architects who straddled the worlds of architecture and movie-set design. It became home to some of the world's great modernist architects who fled Europe between the wars. Some aspects of the playful, colorful design of the first Tomorrowland are reminiscent of work by Charles and Ray Eames. One could also see inspiration from California's Googie architecture and Case Study House program—strong geometries; light, weightless masses; and new and unusual building materials like fiberglass, plastics, and perforated I-Beams.

But among all the other influences, Walt found himself coming back time and time again to amusements in California. One of his favorites was Los Angeles's Beverly Park, which first opened in 1945, and was owned and operated by Dave and Bernice Bradley. Before he became a toolmaker at Lockheed during World War II, Dave started out in show business, managing big-band singer Freddy Martin. Bernice, who was in charge of story research at The Walt Disney Studios, met Dave on the lot at a company party. Bernice described her park to Sam Gennawey, author of *The Disneyland Story*:

Our park was very tiny. There was a carousel, a little train ride, and another little boat ride for children. The boat didn't actually go on water, they simply moved around on the grounds of the park areas. Walt was out there almost every day sitting on the end of the bench, watching how children enjoyed rides.[12]

Arguably one of the most influential fantasy environments that Walt visited during his years of research was Children's Fairyland in Oakland, a 10-acre, $50,000 park built by nursery owner Arthur Navlet (with the support of the city's parks department) on the shores of Lake Merritt in 1950. The park featured costumed guides, fairy-tale sets, farm animals, and live entertainment. There was even an *Alice in Wonderland* attraction, a cartoony castle, and a big blue whale. In fact, Walt hired away their first executive director, Dorothy Manes, a puppeteer, who would remain at Disneyland for 17 years. Perhaps most importantly, Fairyland was home to the paddle-wheel boat that brought the ride designers of Arrow Development into the fold. Although

Walt wasn't impressed with that first boat, he was taken with the custom ride vehicles created by the Northern California firm, and a key early partnership for Disneyland was formed.

Jets, jungles, jangles, and the iron horse

Space Age architecture and wild natural landscapes appear to go hand in hand in Southern California. Author Alan Hess described its Googie coffee shops as a place where "Fred Flintstone and George Jetson could meet over a cup of coffee."[13] The modernism of the area is not cold. It's a sleek jet taking off from a rugged desert airfield or a geodesic dome sprouting out of the wilds of a jungle planet. When Walt later described Adventureland as "Nature's Wonderland," he might have been describing Southern California, a place of natural beauty and wild landscapes. The region is one of the most geographically and biologically diverse places in the world, with an endless variety

OPPOSITE **Nine-year-old Diane Disney tries out the historic bicycles with her dad at the Henry Ford Museum in Dearborn, Michigan, in August 1943. Like Ford, Walt wanted to create a place that captured the development of American culture.**

BELOW **Walt loved taking his daughters, Diane and Sharon, pictured here around 1942, to the merry-go-round in Griffith Park, which was a short distance from their home in the neighborhood of Los Feliz.** *Photo, Earl Theisen*

ABOVE Opened in 1922 and designed
by Hollywood art director Harry Oliver,
the Scottish-themed Tam O'Shanter
in Los Feliz was one of Walt's and
his Imagineers' favorite restaurants.
His regular table was number 31,
and the eatery still has autographed
sketches by studio artists hanging in
its lobby. Oliver's fantasy architecture, which was popular during the
'20s and plentiful in the area, would
influence the designs of buildings
at Disneyland.

OPPOSITE ABOVE The elegant Tivoli
Gardens amusement park in
Copenhagen, Denmark, impressed
Walt, and he took notes for his
own "great, great playground" when
he visited the summer of 1951.
Art, Ib Andersen

OPPOSITE BELOW Walt loved the
elaborately decorated Clifton's
Cafeteria restaurants in Los Angeles.
The tropical-themed "Pacific Seas"
featured ornate stonework and an
exterior waterfall.

"I'm just making notes about something I've always dreamed of, a great, great playground."
—Walt Disney

of flora blooming between the desert and the sea.

Bounded by three mountain ranges, 70 miles of public beach, and deserts stretching into several other states in the Southwest, Southern California boasts such mountain retreats as Walt and Lillian's local vacation spot Lake Arrowhead, and tropical paradises like the exotic gardens of Henry Huntington and Elias Jackson "Lucky" Baldwin, and the Polynesian oasis Don The Beachcomber restaurant in Hollywood (both thematic precursors to the Enchanted Tiki Room at Disneyland).

In addition to movie "ranches" such as the Warner Bros. lot down the street from the Disney Studios in Burbank, and private ranches like the Santa Monica Mountains home of Walt's polo friend Will Rogers, one of Walt's favorite locales was Palm Springs. A popular desert retreat two hours from Los Angeles, Palm Springs is a complete

microcosm that combined Walt's interest in Native American culture with modernist architecture and Western ranch-style living, all in a beautiful natural setting occasionally punctuated with tropical touches. Walt loved the resort city so much that he built a vacation home there at Smoke Tree Ranch, which today still sports horse trails, a community room (named after Walt), and a chuck wagon buffet. Many traditions from Western life live on in Frontierland, and Walt's fondness for Smoke Tree Ranch, in particular, lives on in the "STR" tie he dons in Blaine Gibson's statue of Walt in the hub at Disneyland.

The frontier spirit was also alive at another influential Old West environment in Buena Park: Knott's Berry Farm, just a few miles from where Disneyland would eventually be built. There, Walter Knott and his wife, Cordelia, brought together his popular boysenberry orchard and fruit stand and her chicken dinner restaurant in 1934. Walter would later add buildings for a Ghost Town attraction to entertain folks waiting in line for chicken and biscuits.

In 1952, the same year Walt displayed his Granny's cabin exhibit at the Pan-Pacific Auditorium and determined it was not the way to go, Knott had rescued an old mine train and began the Ghost Town and Calico Railway. Walt directed one of his production designers, Harper Goff, to spend a Sunday afternoon at Knott's examining park operations in December of that year. "The shops and stores were full and people were buying," Goff noted "Particularly in the old-time general store."[14]

Plans for a small park adjacent to the Burbank studio had grown to 16 acres when Walt hired Harper Goff to create drawings in 1951. A year later, two large infrastructure projects (a Los Angeles River flood-control project and the Ventura Freeway expansion plan) threatened the viability of the site, as Walt approached the Burbank City Council with the concept in March 1952:

> *A word may be said in regard to the concept and conduct of Disneyland's operational tone. Although various sections will have the fun and flavor of a carnival or amusement park, there will be none of the pitches, games, wheels, sharp practices and devices designed to milk the visitor's pocketbook. No roller coasters or other rides in the cheap thrill category.*[15]

But the city council wasn't convinced. "We don't want the carny atmosphere in Burbank," proclaimed one lawmaker. "We don't want people falling in the river, or merry-go-rounds squawking all day long."[16] Walt left the meeting and changed course immediately, realizing that even if the project had been approved, it needed more space. He quickly shifted his search elsewhere, but he was determined to have his park in California, home to artists and scientists, engineers and entertainers, the doers and the dreamers. Disneyland was also very much a product of the colossal economic boom in 1950s California. The value of new construction in Los Angeles County for 1953 exceeded that of New York, Chicago, Detroit, Houston, Dallas, Philadelphia, New Orleans, Denver, Baltimore, and Boston combined. California was the natural birthplace for a new kind of revolutionary amusement that would conquer the world with a smile: The Happiest Place on Earth.

ABOVE **When Walt's doctor suggested he take up a hobby after injuries prevented him from playing polo, he began building a miniature railroad he named the Carolwood Pacific Railroad, which took guests around his home on Carolwood Drive in Los Angeles. In his backyard, he constructed a barn where he maintained and built miniature trains. It was moved to Griffith Park in 1999, and is now known as "Walt's Barn."** *Photo, Gene Lester*

FOLLOWING **Before heading off to the dusty trails of Frontierland at Disneyland, Walt test-drives one of the stagecoaches his studio shops built at the Burbank lot in 1954.**

Welcome to Disneyland

To all who come to this happy place: Welcome.

By 1950, Walt Disney had made 472 short films, 13 feature films, won 15 Academy Awards (and been nominated for 18 more), and led a studio with an annual gross income in excess of $2 million and more than 650,000 shares of stock sold;[1] yet he was unable to convince banks, television networks, city officials, nor his own brother that building Disneyland on the parcel adjacent to his studio was a feasible idea. He had to fight for his vision every step of the way. The Burbank City Council didn't trust that the park would be reputable.[2] Banks didn't like the risk of an unproven concept. Architects weren't able to capture the expanse of his imagination. The amusement-park industry thought Walt's extravagance would bankrupt the endeavor.

Undeterred, Walt pulled away from film production and devoted more and more time to his dream project. He was tireless, demanding, selfless, and unrelenting in his goal, even as he was having trouble raising money for it.

Variety reported that the Walt Disney Productions library was worth an estimated $25 million to television,[3] but Walt absolutely refused to license his film library unless he could use it to raise awareness for Disneyland: "If I was ever going to have my park, here, at last, was a way to tell millions of people about it — with TV."[4] His first foray into the burgeoning medium was a 1950 Christmas special on NBC called *One Hour in Wonderland*. Eventually, Walt hoped his stand-alone television experiences of the early 1950s would lead to a series he was planning, simply titled *Disneyland*. In order to acquire the new series, he insisted that a network would have to fund new programming and invest in the park. Although all of the networks were interested in developing a relationship with Walt for access to Disney's existing film library, they didn't have the available capital to fund Walt's proposal, especially after the Federal Communications Committee's freeze on affiliate stations between 1948 and 1952, the networks' major source of income.

And there were even hurdles within the company. His brother Roy, who was now president of Walt Disney Productions, hesitated to fund outside projects after the lean war years. He had allotted $10,000 to research and develop ideas for the park,[5] but Walt needed more. "I couldn't get anybody to go with me because we were going through this financial depression [at the studio]," Walt remembered. "Whenever I'd go down and talk to my brother about it… he'd always suddenly get busy with some figures, so, I mean, I didn't dare bring it up."[6]

Where there is a Walt there is a way

Just when it seemed like everything was working against Walt's plan for the park, Roy came up with an idea. He suggested selling the name "Walt Disney" to the studio and putting Walt on a personal-services contract to enable him to create a separate company to fund the Disneyland project. In addition to an annual royalty of $50,000,

BELOW Once the Anaheim location was selected, Walt invited several Orange County officials to the Disney Studios on December 12, 1954, to share his plans for Disneyland. The group included (left to right) Anaheim Mayor Charles Pearson, Orange County Supervisors Willis Warner and Willard Smith, and Orange County Planning Commission Chairman Dr. W. L. Bigham. *Photo, Willard Smith*

BOTTOM Walt's dreams outgrew his early concept for a 16-acre park between the Burbank studio and Griffith Park. He had approached the Burbank City Council with his idea in March 1952, but the lawmakers feared a "carny atmosphere," and Walt soon realized that he would need more space for the Happiest Place on Earth. *Art, Harper Goff*

Walt now had an option to borrow $50,000 on his company-provided life-insurance policy and the right to make live-action films outside the studio. He also received a licensing fee of $3,000 a week and five to ten percent of merchandising profits.[7] A book and magazine deal with Whitman Publishing (publisher of the Little Golden Books) included a guaranteed loan, and Walt immediately took advantage of the deal.[8] "My wife raised the dickens with me," he recalled. "I spent over $100,000..."[9] He even sold his vacation home in Palm Springs "to get this thing to a point where I could show people what it would be."[10]

As soon as Walt got the money, WED Enterprises (named after his initials, Walter Elias Disney, and later renamed Walt Disney Imagineering in 1986) was incorporated in December 1952. He started recruiting employees: artists and set designers from The Walt Disney Studios, other Hollywood studios, and the carnival business to create a multidisciplinary team that trusted each other and could make decisions quickly. Three months after WED was formed, the

board of directors of Walt Disney Productions agreed to Roy's plan to license Walt's name. "I'm not 'Walt Disney' anymore," Walt told Marty Sklar, who started in publicity and would eventually become president of Walt Disney Imagineering. "Disney is a thing, an attitude, an image in the eyes of the public. I've spent my whole career creating that image, and I am a great believer in what Disney is, but it's not me, the person, anymore."[11]

In April of that year, Disney had approached architects William Pereira and Charles Luckman, who had designed the nearby Marineland park, to submit ideas for his park. Walt wasn't happy with their proposal and turned to his friend and neighbor, architect Welton Becket, for another perspective. Becket politely refused the assignment saying, "Walt, no one can design Disneyland for you. You gotta use your own people. We can't help you. We don't have that kind of a background for this."[12] Walt took his advice: His newly assembled design team at WED would be responsible for designing the entire park.

Bill Cottrell, WED's first employee hired to work on both the park and the *Disneyland* TV show, believed Disneyland was possible because Walt empowered his artists, cartoonists, and executives to develop their skills and talents:

> *Business was slowing down in the studio and instead of laying them off, [Walt] put them on his personal payroll... Walt knew all about the hobbies and outside interests of the men who worked at the studio. So it was no big deal to take men who could turn out a six-minute film short and have them create a three-minute dark ride with visual images.*[13]

Art directors Dick Irvine and Marvin Davis were two of the first to join the team. "We would write our ideas out on squares of paper, put them up on a board, and [Walt] would come down in the afternoon and...juggle them around," Irvine, head of construction and design, remembered. "These sessions would last anywhere from four to six hours, to the entire day."[14]

According to Davis, "Walt would come in at night, just as he used to do with his animators, and take it home with him." When Davis returned to his desk in the morning, Walt would have retraced an entire attraction noting, "Here, quit fooling around and redo this the way it should be."

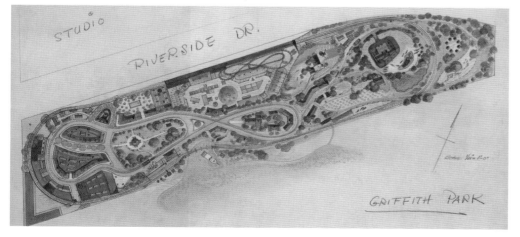

STUDIO

RIVERSIDE DR.

GRIFFITH PARK

DISNEYLAND
SCHEMATIC AERIAL VIEW
APPROX. 45 ACRES
WITHIN RAILROAD TRACKS
· DESIGNED BY WED ENTERPRISES ·

The original Davis tissues reveal this back and forth. Davis added, "You no longer had any big departments to deal with. It was just fun to get back into that small scale again."[15]

Where oh where should my (not so little) park go?

With the Burbank location scrapped, Walt needed land, and a lot of it. Charles Henry "Doc" Strub, builder of the Santa Anita racetrack in nearby Arcadia, suggested that Disneyland be built along the ocean. Walt told him that was the one place where he would not build it.

Architect Charles Luckman suggested that Walt hire Harrison "Buzz" Price with the Stanford Research Institute (SRI) to study potential sites outside of Los Angeles. When they spoke, Walt told Price, "It will be a place for California to be home, to bring guests, to demonstrate its faith in the future."[16] But Price had concerns about the scope. Los Angeles County was more than 4,000 square miles (approximately 10,360 sq km) and greater Los Angeles (which encompassed the counties of Los Angeles, Orange, San Bernardino, Riverside, and Ventura) was more than 35,000 square miles (about 90,650 sq km). Walt would only give Price a budget and timeline: He needed roughly 100 acres (around 41 ha) within the five-county area, and he wanted to open the park

in two years. Beyond that, it was up to Price. The next morning the orders went through to put SRI under contract.

Price studied some 50 major census tracts, looking at weather patterns (including smog) as well as shifting populations, freeway construction, economic factors, and building codes. He considered the sites that would later become Descanso Gardens (nestled in the foothills just northeast of the Burbank studio), Chavez Ravine (future home to Dodger Stadium), Chatsworth (near the rocky grandeur of the Santa Susana Pass State Historic Park near Ventura County), Palos Verdes (home to Marineland), and the Sepulveda Dam area, but determined that Los Angeles was becoming increasingly decentralized. The highest rate of growth was likely to be in Orange County to the south. Focusing on a 150-square-mile (nearly 389 sq km), amoeba-shaped area on either side of the proposed Santa Ana Freeway, SRI identified 10 sites of at least 160 acres (about 65 ha) and recommended Anaheim as his first choice. Walt chose a tract with orange groves and walnut trees. "It was a first-class property. The land was clearly available," Price later said. "We had a good relationship with the city manager of Anaheim, and we could afford it." After one false start, a purchase deal was concluded in August 1953 at $4,500 per acre (4,000 m).[17]

ABOVE **Roy O. Disney traveled to New York in 1953 to sell the concept of the park to financial backers. Walt and artist Herb Ryman, who had worked on such films as** *Dumbo* **and** *The Wizard of Oz,* **spent a weekend together at the studio putting Walt's ideas on paper. "Herbie, this is my dream," the artist remembered Walt telling him tearfully. "I've wanted this for years and I need your help. You're the only one who can do it."** *Art, Herb Ryman*

A new concept IN ENTERTAINMENT!

Walt's friend Art Linkletter remembered being invited for a ride down to the site soon after:

> "It's a deep secret," Walt told me. "You can't tell anybody anything you see or hear." I couldn't believe my eyes… We were driving through orange groves and dirt roads. I didn't tell him what I really thought — that he was out of his mind. After all, it was 45 minutes from where people lived and there was nothing there![18]

The devil is in the details

Walt unveiled the orange-grove property to Marvin Davis and described how the train would define the perimeter, but the key element, the "opening scene" — the entrance, remained. Davis recalled, "I did 129 different schemes for the solution of the thing…until it finally developed into the scheme it is now with the single entrance and the walk for the avenue, which is Main Street, up to the center of the hub."[19] Davis oversaw the architecture for the park and designed attractions including Peter Pan's Flight. Dick Irvine managed the five subdirectors, who were in turn each responsible for a themed land: Harper Goff for Adventureland, Bill Martin for Fantasyland, George Patrick for Frontierland, Wade B. Rubottom for Main Street, and Gabriel Scognamillo for Tomorrowland.

Harper Goff put his experience in the art department at Warner Bros. to good use as the lead designer for Adventureland and had a hand in almost every area of the park. Goff drew inspiration from the historic courthouse from his hometown of Fort Collins, Colorado, for Main Street City Hall. He was tasked with drawing elevations for the Nautilus submarine exhibit in Tomorrowland, because he had created the original for the movie *20,000 Leagues under the Sea* (1954). Ken Anderson remembered how his crew was still painting the giant squid for the *20,000 Leagues* exhibit shortly before the park opened, when Walt — who had left a VIP preview dinner to check ongoing work — found them, put on a mask, and started painting himself.

Through their experience designing for the park, "two 'partners' from animation background painting days at the Disney studio, Claude Coats and John Hench, became the world's foremost designers of three-dimensional show spaces,"[20] according to Sklar. Hench was very influential in creating the Disney theme park vernacular. "We called him the good taste merchant," says designer Rolly Crump. "Everything he did was in good taste."[21] Coats reworked the design of each Fantasyland ride to match the emotional mood of the very same movies for which he had painted scenes, including *Snow White and the Seven Dwarfs* and *Peter Pan*. He was later instrumental on "it's a small world," Carousel of Progress, Susbmarine Voyage, the Haunted Mansion, Pirates of the Caribbean, and more. Hench used color, viewpoint, and character development to tell a wide variety of stories, from the thrilling Tomorrowland *Moonliner* rocket to the exotic Enchanted Tiki Room.

The Stanford Research Institute hosted more than 150 design charrettes to analyze the amusement-park business. One workshop, held in November during the 1953

National Association of Amusement Parks, Pools, and Beaches convention, included the leaders of Chicago's Riverview Park, New Orleans' Pontchartrain Beach Amusement Park, Cincinnati's Coney Island, and San Francisco's Playland at the Beach. After two hours of presentations, which included caviar and an open bar, Price recalled the reaction was unanimous: "Mr. Disney's park idea is too expensive to build and too expensive to operate."[22] Attendees also complained about the attractions:

> *Custom rides will never work. They will cost too much to buy and they will be constantly breaking down…Only stock off-the-shelf rides are cheap enough and reliable enough to do the job…the public doesn't know the difference or care.…[the] proven moneymakers are conspicuously missing, no roller coasters, no Ferris wheel…no tunnel of love…no beer.… Without [carney] barkers to sell sideshows, the marks wouldn't pay to go*

> *in…Things like the castle and the pirate ship are cute, but they aren't rides, so there's no economic reason to build them. There is too much wasteful landscaping …The interior finishing concepts of the restaurants are too expensive…*[23]

Their concerns were summed up with this statement: "People will vandalize the ride vehicles and destroy the grounds no matter what you do, so you may as well go cheap."[24] Walt wasn't dissuaded; he didn't want to create just another amusement park, he had bigger plans.

Racing to the finish line
Armed with a site and a design team, Walt still couldn't get a television network to sponsor it. In September 1953, Roy paid a visit to Bank of America in New York to ask for a loan and to again approach ABC now that he had *Snow White and the Seven Dwarfs* sequence director Bill Cottrell's outline for the *Disneyland* television series. Walt

LEFT Imagineers Harriet Burns, Claude Coats, and Fred Joerger work on a candy-covered model of the Rock Candy Mountain attraction, which was planned for Fantasyland in 1957 but never built. "Fred would help me paint props," Burns recalled. "And then if Fred was in a bind, I would help him on the models." A replica inspired by the original model can be viewed in the window of Trolley Treats at Disney California Adventure Park.

BELOW Many of the same artists who worked on the animated feature films designed the painted backgrounds for the Disneyland attractions. Mr. Toad's Wild Ride was adapted from the 1949 film *The Adventures of Ichabod and Mr. Toad*.

40

ABOVE Walt discusses the model of
Sleeping Beauty Castle with his
Imagineers. It was displayed at the
Los Angeles County Fair in the fall of
1954, along with a Disneyland map,
to promote the upcoming *Disneyland*
television show on ABC, which
debuted on October 27 of that year.
Photo, Earl Thiesen

BELOW Renié Conley, Academy Award–winning costume designer for *Cleopatra*, was hired by Walt in 1954 to design costumes—10,000 of them—for Disneyland personnel for the park's opening day. *Art, Renié Conley*

OPPOSITE Peter Ellenshaw was a special-effects artist, matte painter, and production designer for movies including *Treasure Island* and *20,000 Leagues Under the Sea*. While at Disney Studios, Walt also had him work on the design of such Disneyland attractions as TWA's Rocket to the Moon.

knew by now that words alone would not be enough—he needed a spectacular piece of art to show the executives the master plan for what his magical land would look like.

Walt approached Herb Ryman, a painter and illustrator, who had worked with the studio on *Dumbo* (1941) and with Cedric Gibbons at Metro-Goldwyn-Mayer on *Mutiny on the Bounty* (1935) and *The Wizard of Oz* (1939) to create the plan, but Ryman would only agree if Walt worked at his side. On the weekend of September 26, 1953, with Roy standing by in New York, the duo scrapped Harper Goff's Burbank plans and started over. Together they combined the ideas that had been percolating with Marvin Davis and his team that summer. Disneyland would be a magical metropolis with themed lands radiating from a central-plaza hub. The pair finished the rendering of the park just in time for it to be flown to Roy for his meeting with Bank of America.

Though the rendering was spectacular, as late as February 1954 (five months before construction began on the park) there was still no deal. NBC continued to stall. CBS stood up Disney's representative. Leonard Goldenson of ABC remembered it was his

idea to address the network's board. New York banks wouldn't fund Disney directly and wouldn't fund ABC to fund Disney, so Goldenson decided to personally arrange the financing. He asked old colleague Karl Hoblitzelle, a wealthy Texas oil baron, theater owner, and the chairman of Republic Bank, to underwrite a $5 million loan.[25]

On April 2, 1954, the boards of ABC and Walt Disney Productions approved a deal that included stock, bonds, and guaranteed loans that gave ABC almost 35 percent ownership of the park. After ABC's investment, Bank of America increased Disney's credit line to $8 million.[26] That same day, plans for the construction of Disneyland were announced to the public. Walt needed to be everywhere at once, traveling from the studio to WED to the construction site, so in July he set up a personal helicopter service and drew a landing pad into the plans.[27] With the construction of Main Street, Walt had a personal apartment included in the plans above the fire station. From this vantage point he could look out onto the progress of the park. A lamp still burns in the window today, illuminated in honor of Walt's lasting legacy.[28]

When ground was broken on July 21, 1954, there were only 257 working days until the scheduled opening of the park. Farmhouses on the site were repurposed for construction management. Cornelius Vanderbilt ("C. V.") Wood, who worked at SRI with Buzz Price, was appointed construction manager for the Disneyland project; Charles Alexander was the construction field supervisor; and George Mills was the foreman for the on-site mills and shops. Admiral Joe Fowler, a former Navy man coaxed away from building subdivisions, was responsible for Disneyland construction contracts, including prime contractor McNeil Construction, which had built the 1926 Orpheum Theatre in Los Angeles, the 1956 Lockheed missile plant in Palo Alto, and the 1955 Dunes Hotel in Las Vegas. McNeil would be responsible for clearing the site, excavating lakes and rivers, installing utilities, and building the railroad bed and berm that surrounds the park.

McNeil set about grading the site while families were still moving off their farm properties. Dirt excavated from the rivers created the berm. Many of the farms operated off the grid and more than a mile and a half (about 2.4 km) of clay pipe was laid for the sewer system alone. In September 1954, the city of Anaheim voted to annex the 800 acres (approximately 324 ha) surrounding Disneyland, allowing the connection to city services. A construction supervisor recalled his pride as water flowed into the Rivers of America in Frontierland for the first time, and then the immediate disappointment as he watched it disappear into the sandy soil. Clay was brought in to waterproof the leaking riverbed.

Meanwhile, Roy worked to procure sponsorships for the *Disneyland* TV series, even offering partial ownership of the show to big companies like Coca-Cola if they would also set up shop in the park. But the big break came through engineer and developer C. V. Wood. The 33-year-old "was the quickest numbers man I ever had for a client," Price recalled.[29] Wood secured Chicago meatpacker Swift & Co. to operate the Market House on Main Street, and that success opened the floodgates to 40 other sponsorships, including the Santa Fe Railroad Company, Bank of America, Richfield Oil, Upjohn, and Carnation. Sponsors built out their own shops with required exhibition space, and their rental fees generated much needed income.

Disneyland premiered on October 27, 1954, as one of the first original television series produced by a movie studio. The extraordinarily successful programming featured Disney movies; appearances by Mouseketeers; 30-minute *World of Tomorrow* segments, with updates from Bell Laboratories and the aerospace industry; *Adventureland*, featuring *True-Life Adventures* nature documentaries and new productions like the Emmy Award–winning *Davy Crockett* serial; and ongoing progress reports from the site in Anaheim. Time-lapse cameras were set up in special towers built solely to document construction, which was featured on the television show. All of America was glued to their television sets, transfixed by the park taking shape, eagerly awaiting their chance to step into the fantasy. And Disneyland needed all the publicity it could get.

"Walt, no one can design Disneyland for you. You gotta use your own people."
—Welton Becket

"*I couldn't believe my eyes... We were driving through orange groves and dirt roads. I didn't tell him what I really thought — that he was out of his mind. After all, it was 45 minutes from where people lived and there was nothing there!*"

—Art Linkletter

OPPOSITE In less than a year, 160 acres of orange and walnut trees would be transformed into Main Street, U.S.A., Tomorrowland, and Sleeping Beauty Castle.

OPPOSITE "I want you to work on Disneyland...and you are going to like it!" Walt told animator John Hench, who had worked on *Fantasia* and *Dumbo*. And Hench did like it. Pictured here with Walt at his Burbank office during the park's early planning stages, Hench explained that at Disneyland they had the opportunity to achieve what they did in the animated films "in another way—three-dimensional." *Photo, Alfred Eisenstaedt*

RIGHT "I want a hub at the end of Main Street," Walt told Imagineer Herb Ryman as they were planning the layout of the park. "From where the other lands will radiate, like the spokes of a wheel...Disneyland is going to be a place where you can't get lost or tired unless you want to." *Art, Marvin Davis*

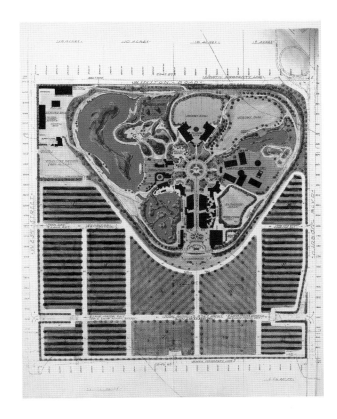

> ## "Walt always wanted something no one else had."
>
> — Bob Gurr

Watching a dream grow

Come early December, the crew poured the foundation and erected the frame of the Opera House, the first structure built at the park. Due to the speed of construction, grading was still happening while the buildings were being surveyed and staked. Tomorrowland wasn't graded until the following month, so Goff started using scale models to assist with layout, replacing stakes laid by surveyors with those he "eyeballed." On March 5, 1955, the city of Anaheim issued a building permit for the construction of the castle. Even on tight schedules, Walt insisted on perfection, repainting Main Street storefronts when they didn't look right and adding more elaborate gingerbread trim. At the train station he ordered workmen to recrush the ballast rock to match the 5:8 scale of his railroad.

Foliage had a starring role at Disneyland, as much a nature park as a small city,

containing vast landscaped areas. "Walt Disney depleted our nurseries from Santa Barbara to San Diego," the infamous Hollywood columnist Hedda Hopper wrote at the time.[30] Walt told one reporter that more than a half-million dollars went into trees and shrubbery alone, including three giant palms saved from the original homes on the site. Jack and Morgan "Bill" Evans were responsible for the exotic foliage of the park. Bill recalled Walt's requests:

> *He made specific comments only if something didn't exactly suit his idea. I planted a Brazilian pepper tree near the walk just past Adventureland. It had a big heavy trunk, and its spread was about 30 feet [about 9 m]. As we were parading through the park one Saturday morning, Walt stopped and looked back at the tree and said he thought it was too close to the walk. The next morning we put in another crew, boxed up the six-ton [about 5 t] root system, and moved the tree about six feet [1.8 m]. The next Saturday morning Walt walked right past it. No comment.[31]*

In February 1955, Welton Becket recommended landscape architect Ruth Shellhorn to create designs for Main Street, Tomorrowland, and the castle courtyard. Soon after she began, Walt quickly expanded her scope to encompass areas of the other themed lands.

The complexity of the project and the number of tradesmen and unions combined with the condensed construction schedule had everyone scrambling to finish on time. During the final weeks the size of the construction crew tripled to 2,500 workers, many putting in double shifts. The crane operators worked in rotating shifts around the clock to complete work, which included lifting animatronic animals into the Jungle Cruise river. In May, Orange County plumbers and asphalt workers went on strike. When they returned Walt paid higher wages retroactively so the union plumbers would prioritize the installation of restrooms. As opening day approached, control centers, loudspeakers, and complex ride systems equipment were still being hidden all over the park.

Back at WED headquarters, craftsmen were testing the "dark rides" and building mock-ups and models. A customized 1922 merry-go-round, the King Arthur Carrousel, was purchased in Toronto, and construction began on a pair of steam locomotives

for the Santa Fe and Disneyland Railroad. Earl Vilmer led the railroad team under Roger Broggie, head of the machine shop, who had started at the studio in 1939 helping to install the multiplane camera. Others in this group included Ed Lingenfelter, who after spending a career designing steam locomotives in Pennsylvania, was hired out of retirement by Walt to engineer the 5:8 scale Disney locomotive. Model railroader Eddie Sergeant was brought on to draft up all the railroad cars and then the Main Street horse-drawn streetcars in August 1954. Dick Bagley drafted the steam engines for the Mark Twain Riverboat, and Bob Gurr had his hands on every vehicle in the park.

"During these redesign sessions I got a chance to work with Karl Bacon and Ed Morgan of Arrow Development," Gurr remembered. "They built a lot of the Disney ride machines over the years. They were never upset that Roger Broggie had me redesigning their products. We were both interested in getting it right for Walt."[32] Bacon did the theoretical work, calculations, and technological innovations. Morgan could turn concepts into working rides and was the face of the company. He remembered the hands-on way Walt worked:

We were at the studio in Burbank… early one morning for a meeting… Walt Disney drives up… He had a bathrobe on and pajamas on under it… He comes in and lies down on the floor. Walt stretches out and puts his hands under his head. He's asking questions and conducting this meeting. I was down on the floor beside him and was explaining things to him![33]

In the weeks leading up to opening day, thousands of cars had to be turned away at the gate. Traffic officers were doubled and the United States Marine Corps took aerial photos of the area to help determine how to handle the loads.

Storming the castle

In the end, most of the park was finished in time for the ribbon-cutting ceremony, even though the drinking fountains were dry and the asphalt was still a little soft. After almost two decades of planning and delays, a backbreaking year of construction, and an investment of $17 million,[34] opening day was here — Sunday, July 17, 1955. The Invitational Press Preview of Disneyland was attended not only by invited press and VIPs, but thousands of gatecrashers, and a

OPPOSITE **During the construction of the park, Walt sometimes traveled from his Burbank studio to Anaheim via helicopter. The park later hosted a landing pad for the original VIP experience at the Disneyland Hotel across the street from the amusement park.**

ABOVE **Visitors lounge in a 1956 Dodge Custom Royal by the gates of Disneyland.** *Photo, Maurice Terrell*

MAIN STREET

ATTRACTIONS AND AMUSEMENTS

1 Grand Canyon Diorama • Horse-drawn Streetcars • Main Street Railroad Station • Santa Fe & Disneyland Railroad (Main Line: Excursion Train, Passenger Train, Western Freight Train)
2 Horse-drawn Surreys
3 Double-decked Omnibus • 1904 Horseless Carriages
4 Penny Arcade
6 Main Street Cinema
10 Plaza Dancing Area

SPECIAL SHOWS AND EXHIBITS

4 Upjohn Pharmacy (Apothecary)
6 Yale & Towne (Locks & Keys) Swift's Market House • Wurlitzer Music Hall (Pianos & Organs)

SHOPS AND STORES

2 Global Locker Service • News Stands
3 Main Street Music • Mickey Mouse Club Shop • Hat Shop
4 Books, Children • Candle Shop Emporium Department Store • Glass Blower • Flower Mart
5 Candy Palace
6 Jewelry Shop • Magic Shop • Market House • Tobacco Shop • Print Shop
7 Camera Store • Hallmark Cards Silhouette Studio • Watch Shop (Timex) • China & Glass
8 Mad Hatter Hats

FOOD AND REFRESHMENTS

1 Refreshment Stand (Railroad Station)
3 Hills Bros. Coffee House and Coffee Garden
5 Ice Cream Parlor (Carnation Co.) Citrus House (Sunkist)
8 Disneyland Plaza Pavilion (Self Service) Refreshment Corner (Coca-Cola Co.)
10 Carnation Plaza Gardens (Open Air)
11 Red Wagon Restaurant (Swift & Co.)

SPECIAL SERVICES

3 Bank of America
7 Hallmark Cards Communication Center Eastman Kodak Camera Exhibit and Photo Information Headquarters
9 Baby Station Carefree Corner (North America Information Center)
12 Ken-L-Land (Dog and Cat "Motel") Stroller and Wheel Chairs

▲ FRONTIERLAND

ATTRACTIONS AND AMUSEMENTS

1 Columbia 1790 Sailing Ship • Mark Twain Sternwheel Riverboat
2 Western Mine Train and Mule Pack through Nature's Wonderland
3 Frontier Shooting Gallery
6 Mike Fink Keelboats • Tom Sawyer Island and Raft Ride • Western Railroad Station (Main Line)
7 Indian War Canoes • Indian Village

SPECIAL SHOWS AND EXHIBITS

4 Pepsi-Cola Golden Horseshoe Revue
7 Indian Village Ceremonial Dances

Disneyland Hotel and Gourmet Restaurant

Monorail Station

FOOD AND REFRESHMENTS

2 Casa de Fritos (Mexican Food)
4 Golden Horseshoe (Pepsi-Cola) Malt Shop • Oaks Tavern
5 Aunt Jemima's Kitchen (Pancakes)
8 Tom Sawyer Island Refreshment Stand (Nesbitt's)

SHOPS AND STORES

2 Hat Shop
3 Bone Jewelry • Pendleton Woolen Mills Shop • Mexican Village Trading Post • Gem Shop • Curio Hut
4 Frontier Gun Shop
7 Indian Shop

◆ FANTASYLAND

ATTRACTIONS AND AMUSEMENTS

1 Sleeping Beauty Castle Walk-through
2 Casey Jr. Train • Dumbo the Flying Elephant • Skyway Ride to Tomorrowland • Snow White Adventures • Fantasyland Theatre
3 Alice in Wonderland Adventures Mr. Toad's Wild Ride • Peter Pan Flight • Storybook Land Canal Boat Ride
4 Super Autopia Freeways (Richfield Oil Co.) • Motor Boat Cruise Railroad Station (Main Line) Midget Autopia
5 Carrousel • Mad Hatter Tea Party Ride

SHOPS AND STORES

1 Clock Shop • Castle Candy Kitchen • Magic Shop • Tinker Bell Toy Shop
2 The Art Corner, Gifts
3 Mad Hatter Hats

FOOD AND REFRESHMENTS

2 Grape Juice Stand (Welch's)
3 Food & Refreshment Stands
5 Pirate Ship Restaurant (Chicken of the Sea) In Skull Rock Cove

■ TOMORROWLAND

ATTRACTIONS AND AMUSEMENTS

2 The Art of Animation
3 20,000 Leagues Under the Sea Exhibit
4 Rocket to the Moon (Douglas Aircraft Co.) Astro Jet
5 Super Autopia Freeway (Richfield) Skyway Ride to Fantasyland • Railroad Station (Main Line) • Space Bar Dance Area
6 Submarine Voyage (General Dynamics Display) • Disneyland-Alweg Monorail System
7 The Matterhorn (Bobsled Runs)
8 Flying Saucers

record-breaking 90 million viewers on ABC. More than half the country tuned in to view *Dateline Disneyland*, the live ABC special remote broadcast hosted by Art Linkletter and actors Bob Cummings and Ronald Reagan. It was the largest such production ever attempted, requiring 24 cameras spread throughout the park and hundreds of technicians. Producer Sherman Marks had to borrow personnel from other networks and cameras from as far away as Chicago. The complex broadcast was, according to central director Harold Eisenstein, the "biggest engineering feat on television up to that time."

Roy O. Disney spent the first dollar at Disneyland. His admission ticket offered entrance to the park, but enjoying an attraction required additional tickets. Coupon books were introduced that fall. An "A" ticket with a face value of 10 cents was good for several rides, including the vintage merry-go-round-turned-carousel. A "B" ticket was listed for 25 cents and offered thrills like the Mad Tea Party. For a showstopper like Jungle Cruise,

you needed a "C" ticket. The stakes went even higher with the debut of the "D" tickets in 1956 and "E" tickets topping out at 75 cents in 1959.

Guests used their tickets that first day to ride the Santa Fe and Disneyland Railroad around the park with stops on Main Street and Frontierland. Near the Main Street station they could board a horse-drawn streetcar, ride in a surrey, watch a silent movie at the Main Street Cinema, play a game in the Penny Arcade, hear music in the Wurlitzer Music Hall, and visit the Eastman Kodak camera shop, the Upjohn Pharmacy exhibit, or the Emporium. They could have a bite at the Red Wagon Inn, the Coca-Cola Refreshment corner, or the Carnation Ice Cream Parlor, or listen to the Firehouse Five Plus Two play. Choreographer Miriam Nelson sent dancers to perform in each land as the TV cameras rolled. Walt read his dedication, knights lowered the drawbridge, and a surging crowd of ecstatic children ran through the gates of Fantasyland.

> **"We hope that it will be unlike anything else on this earth: a fair, amusement park, an exhibition, a city from the Arabian Nights, a metropolis of the future; in fact, a place of hopes and dreams, facts and fancy, all in one."**
>
> —**Walt Disney**

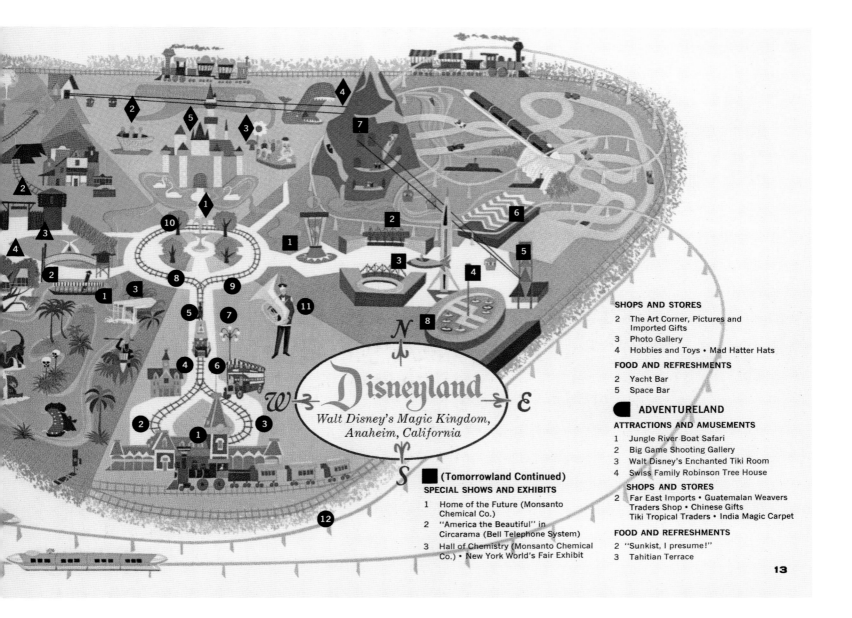

SHOPS AND STORES

2   The Art Corner, Pictures and
    Imported Gifts
3   Photo Gallery
4   Hobbies and Toys • Mad Hatter Hats

FOOD AND REFRESHMENTS

2   Yacht Bar
5   Space Bar

■ ADVENTURELAND

ATTRACTIONS AND AMUSEMENTS

1   Jungle River Boat Safari
2   Big Game Shooting Gallery
3   Walt Disney's Enchanted Tiki Room
4   Swiss Family Robinson Tree House

SHOPS AND STORES

2   Far East Imports • Guatemalan Weavers
    Traders Shop • Chinese Gifts
    Tiki Tropical Traders • India Magic Carpet

FOOD AND REFRESHMENTS

2   "Sunkist, I presume!"
3   Tahitian Terrace

(Tomorrowland Continued)

SPECIAL SHOWS AND EXHIBITS

1   Home of the Future (Monsanto
    Chemical Co.)
2   "America the Beautiful" in
    Circarama (Bell Telephone System)
3   Hall of Chemistry (Monsanto Chemical
    Co.) • New York World's Fair Exhibit

13

Other opening attractions included Peter Pan's Flight, Mad Tea Party, Mr. Toad's Wild Ride, Dumbo the Flying Elephant,[35] Canal Boats of the World, and Snow White's Adventures as well as Merlin's Magic Shop. In Tomorrowland guests could ride Autopia, or visit Space Station X-1, the Art Corner, or the Monsanto Hall of Chemistry. At Circarama, U.S.A., visitors could watch *A Tour of the West*, a special 360-degree travelogue film projected on multiple screens. Later that summer guests could fly model planes in the Flight Circle or eat at the Yacht Bar. Adventureland offered the Jungle Cruise, dining at the Plaza Pavilion, and shopping at the Marketplace. Frontierland guests could ride the Stage Coach, Mule Pack, or the Mark Twain Riverboat, or visit the Indian Village, see a show in the Golden Horseshoe, or sit down for a chicken dinner at Swift's Plantation House.

Some of the attractions that were open, however, still had kinks to work out. The Dumbo the Flying Elephant vehicles were some of the most problematic. An engineer at Arrow realized that tweaking the lubrication would make a more energy-efficient ride mechanism, but his early attempt was throwing the ride out of alignment and spewing foam everywhere. "We used a man by the name of Paul Harvey on site. We left him down there to…milk the elephants!" remembered Karl Bacon. "While they were loading, he'd go out there and drain the system and put in clean oil."[36] Said Morgan: "We were running back and forth to the surplus store 'til 10 at night."[37] But they kept the ride running.

Two of the biggest complaints on opening day were the hot weather and large crowds. And the heat of that July day wasn't just experienced by thirsty guests. "The day was getting hotter and hotter," said Bob Gurr, who was in charge of the Autopia cars driving in formation for the parade down Main Street. "And all the cars began to vapor lock after idling in the heat for 15 minutes. Just as the cars were to join the parade, I ran madly

ABOVE **A map from a 1963 souvenir guidebook shows Disneyland's many attractions. One of its designers, John Hench, shared what he believed was the secret to its magic: "When you go to Disneyland, there is no horizon—just Disneyland....the environment is very special because nothing leaks in from outside."**

Although Roy O. Disney purchased ticket #0001, the first paying guest through the gates was 22-year-old college student Dave MacPherson, who had lined up before 1 A.M. on opening day, July 17, 1955. Even though some attractions were barely functional, "There really was no way to stop and rebuild things during that first summer season," said Imagineer Bob Gurr. "Just weld and fix, weld and fix."

from car to car to restart the stalled engines." But the high temperatures didn't stop the droves of citizens who started showing up well before 2:30 P.M., the earliest start time on the tickets. An estimated 10,000 to 15,000 guests were invited to the park, but twice as many people showed up. Some tickets had a blank space where you could write in how many people were in your party, and some added astronomical numbers.

Much has also been made of the unfinished nature of Disneyland on its opening

day, so much so that Marty Sklar recalled that it took on the name "Black Sunday." Roped-off areas featured "TO BE OPEN SOON" signs or models and renderings of upcoming attractions. The mechanical difficulties combined with closed attractions resulted in unbearable wait times. "If the number of functioning cars dwindled," Gurr remembered, the line "got longer and longer. Guests were jumping the fence running up the track and commandeering the returning cars."

Sklar remembered overhearing guest interactions at the ticket booths: "'I want to go on the Jungle Cruise, the Rocket to the Moon, and the Mark Twain Riverboat —but I don't want to go on any rides!'… In [customers'] minds the whips, shoot-the-chutes, whirligig, and lose-your-lunch thrills of those amusements parks were the rides—which Disneyland did not have." The wide-open, parklike atmosphere might have been hard to appreciate in the chaos of opening day, but guests would soon come to love it.

It took some time to counteract some of the initial negative press, including H. W. Mooring's *Los Angeles Tidings* review, which stated, "Walt's dream is a nightmare, a fiasco the like of which I cannot recall in thirty years of show life."[38] Or the *Los Angeles Mirror News*: "Crowds gripe over long waiting lines everywhere — Disneyland, Orange County's new $17 million playground, was the land of gripes and complaints again today, as a huge, milling throng of 48,000 people had the place bulging at the seams."[39] But syndicated columnist Sheila Graham was the most prescient: "to sum up, Disneyland was a disappointment…but don't be discouraged, boys and girls — Walt Disney has always been a smart trader, and I'm sure there'll be some changes made."[40]

Disneyland public relations director Ed Ettinger and publicity manager Eddie Meck spent the summer inviting reporters back for early dinners at the Red Wagon Inn or the Plantation House followed by a guided tour of the park. The tactic worked, as evidenced in a follow-up story in the *Mirror News*: "If you're planning a trip to Disneyland, go out in the late afternoon…Lines everywhere moved swiftly, with only brief waits…In my opinion, the entire park looks more captivating by night than day."[41]

With the media appeased and opening-day glitches resolved, the crowds kept growing. Gurr might have summed up the first summer the best:

> *Some of the refinements were easy to implement, like where shade is needed, how queue lines should work, and how ride operators can be trained to handle almost any human situation…There really was no way to stop and rebuild things during that first summer season. Just weld and fix, weld and fix, long-term improvements would have to wait until fall when all our young guests were back in school and we could catch our breath.*[42]

By the fall, most of the attractions from the first wave were now open, and special guests from royalty to the Hollywood elite who were arriving via helicopter soon had their own pad at the Disneyland Hotel, which opened on October 5. The long and low modernist Disneyland Hotel echoed the desert resorts of Las Vegas and was designed by Pereira and Luckman. Financed and operated by developer Jack Wrather and his wife, actress Bonita Granville, the 30-acre (roughly 12 ha), $10 million hotel[43] combined the luxury of full service with the indoor-outdoor living of Southern California, boasting day care, three swimming pools, a putting course for golfers,[44] the 1,200-seat Gourmet restaurant, and rooms overlooking grounds designed by landscape architect Raymond E. Page.

Los Angeles theater architect S. Charles Lee was fond of saying, "The show starts on the sidewalk," and it most certainly did at Disneyland. There was the iconic flagpole sign on Harbor Boulevard, and guests arriving by car parked in the 100-acre (about 41 ha) lot before boarding a futuristic tram to the park. Cast members could load 12,000 vehicles with assembly-line precision. Said Gurr, "Walt always wanted something no one else had."

Disneyland
Hotel
and RESTAURANTS
INFORMAL DRESS
REDUCED
WINTER RATES
SPECIAL PACKAGE PLAN
SUNDAY TO WED
ALSO
INCLUDES ROOM TWO MEALS
PARK ADMISSION TEN RIDES
AIRPORT LIMOUSINE SERVICE HERE

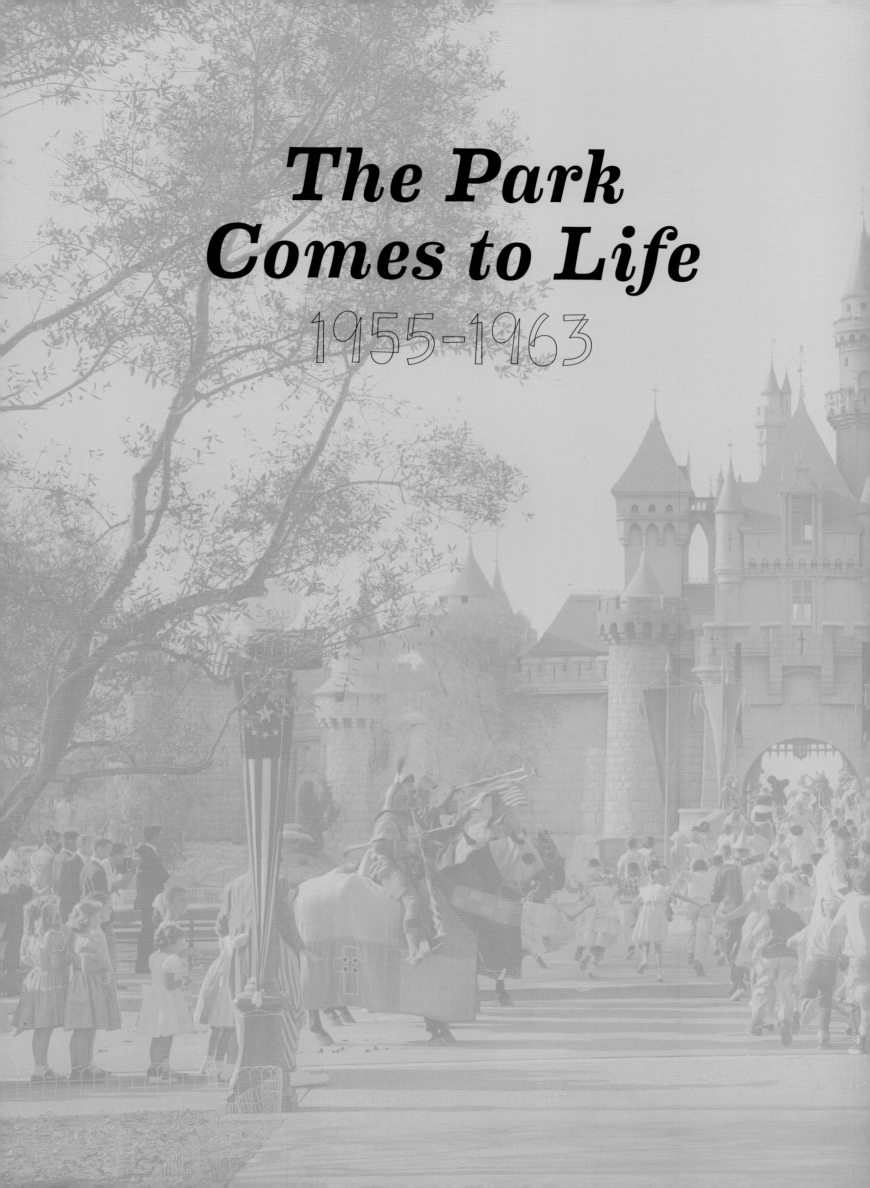

The Park
Comes to Life
1955-1963

Main Street, U.S.A.

*Here, age relives
fond memories of the past…*

"When we began designing Disneyland, we looked at it just the way we do a motion picture. We had to tell a story, or in this case, a series of stories," one designer recalled. "But in Disneyland, we had more control. We designed the entire park so that a guest couldn't miss Scene One or Scene Two. From the moment he entered our 'theatre,' that is our front gate, Scene One would begin for him."[1]

Just past the Disneyland turnstiles a smiling Mickey Mouse greets guests, one made of bright seasonal flowers, including dwarf pink phlox,[2] as specified by landscape architect Ruth Shellhorn. On each side of the garden are entrance tunnels carved from a 20-foot-high, densely landscaped earthen berm that surrounds the park, with the railroad running along the top. Walt understood the power of berms. Bill Evans and his brother, Jack, who landscaped much of the park according to Shellhorn's master plans, had earlier installed a berm at The Walt Disney Studios in Burbank, then another at Walt's Holmby Hills home. "I built that thing up on the canyon," Walt recalled, "so when I was down there playing with my friends, my neighbors wouldn't be annoyed."[3] The berm at the park blocks the outside world visually, aurally, and emotionally.

As visitors walk down the tunnels, they experience darkness for a moment before the show begins. "Walt wanted the guests to enter this land under hypnosis," said Imagineer Herb Ryman. "A magical place where they could not see anything of the outside world."[4]

Art director Dick Irvine remembered visiting other amusement parks and high-traffic locations with Walt: "We measured the width of the walkways and traffic flow, and studied how people moved about."[5] Walt said, "Disneyland is a place [where] you can't get lost or tired unless you want to."[6] Design elements like connecting shop interiors and bright, high-contrast colors used on the Main Street facades worked as "visual incentives to entice guests to move"[7] forward and toward the Central Plaza.

Inspired by the radial street plan of Paris, with the étoile becoming the junction and the castle standing in for the Arc de Triomphe,[8] Walt envisioned this hub as the "heart of Disneyland." The lands radiate out from the center like the spokes of a wheel. Or as Walt described it, "like the four cardinal points of the compass, Disneyland is divided into four cardinal realms."[9] From any point it is easy to get back to the hub, gather together for a moment, and choose your next adventure.

Animator-turned-art director John Hench borrowed a film term to describe Walt: "the inventor of the three-dimensional cross dissolve."[10] To avoid an abrupt change from one themed land into another, subtle changes ease the transition. As guests walk into Adventureland, walkways change from concrete to cut stone, and wrought-iron railings morph into bamboo to cue guests for the next journey. The Pavillion (later

PREVIOUS **A fairy tale come true: Mounted knights step aside as kids storm Sleeping Beauty Castle in Fantasyland on opening day. Crowds of 15,000 people were expected to attend the festivities, but more than 28,000 entered the park's gates on July 17, 1955.**

OPPOSITE **A Denver schoolgirl sends postcards to friends back home from Main Street, U.S.A., in 1957.**

ABOVE This view, from the Main Street station toward the castle, shows the Emporium on the left and Wurlitzer Music Hall (under scaffolding) on the right. WED Enterprises was able to create an immersive turn-of-the-century environment by combining detailed architectural facades with "authentic mementos of the gay and glamorous 90's" inside. Historic artifacts included the stained-glass ceiling from a St. James Park mansion in Los Angeles, which was installed in the Red Wagon Inn. *Photo, Delmar Watson*

OPPOSITE In 1948, Walt visited the historic sites at Colonial Williamsburg in Virginia where costumed docents portrayed everyday life in the 18th century. This trip would most inspire him to create his own turn-of-the-century town. Antique gas lamps were sourced from all over the country to bring early 20th-century authenticity to Main Street, U.S.A., depicted here in artwork that appeared in a Disneyland newspaper supplement in 1955. Baltimore was one of the last places where they were in regular use until the city replaced more than 10,000 of them a few months before Disneyland opened.

renamed the Plaza Pavilion) is an example of visual storytelling on a grander scale. The facade facing Main Street sports a Victorian mansard roof dripping with lacy ironwork, a deep porch, and finials galore, while the facade facing Adventureland is a thatched A-frame. And the stockade fence of Frontierland continues just far enough into Adventureland to conceal a restroom.

Everything old is new again

In the 1950s, suburban shopping malls pulled customers away from the authentic historic downtowns of America, which were rapidly going extinct. Main Street's turn-of-the-century setting, romanticized as a gentler time, contributes to different expectations of behavior, drawing the visitor into a lost world. Disneyland itself is just as old today as the setting of Main Street, U.S.A., was when it opened. The corner drugstore and the barbershop quartet were within living memory.

The interiors of buildings on Main Street are filled with authentic antiques and meticulously crafted replicas made at the studio under the art direction of Wade B. Rubottom, who had worked on the 1940 films *The Philadelphia Story* and *The Shop Around the Corner*. Hench noted:

Only a few historical sources were available to tell us about surface finishes and furnishings in American small town Main Streets....We found few books, few reproduction period wallpapers or carpets, and even fewer craftsmen who could do period work. It took painstaking research to provide Main Street with the authentic details it needed.[11]

A team including Bill Martin and Bill Cottrell was sent to take measurements of New York's Fifth Avenue, Washington's National Mall, and New Orleans' French Quarter, as well as the gas lamps and cobblestone streets at the Chicago Museum of Science and Industry's new exhibit "Yesterday's Main Street." It took three cities to provide the 100 year-old gas streetlamps that lined Main Street, U.S.A.,[12] and each night lamplighters set them aglow.[13]

Builders balked at Walt's insistence on authenticity. "I wanted to put plastic railing up on top of the houses on Main Street," said construction supervisor C. V. Wood. "[Walt] wanted real wrought iron 40 feet [about 12 m] in the air."[14] Even the tiniest details were important according to Hench: "Walt knew that if details are missing or incorrect, you

Building labels: BLDG No. 504   BLDG. No. 505   ELEVATION. 506   BLDG No. 507   BLDG No

500 BLK.

ABOVE Forced perspective was used to make the buildings of Main Street, U.S.A., appear taller in 1955 concept art. Building the upper levels at a progressively smaller scale than the ground level creates the effect.

BELOW Clear visual storytelling is key in designing an authentic and idealized environment: one that is calming, emotionally directive, and effectively creates the feeling of stepping into another world.

#11

BLDG. NO. 509

ELEV.

#9

BLDG. NO. 510

BLDG. NO. 511

BLDG. NO. 512

BLDG. NO. 513

BELOW Engineer and chief developer of Disneyland, C. V. Wood, helped secure the first sponsored spot on Main Street: Swift's Market House.

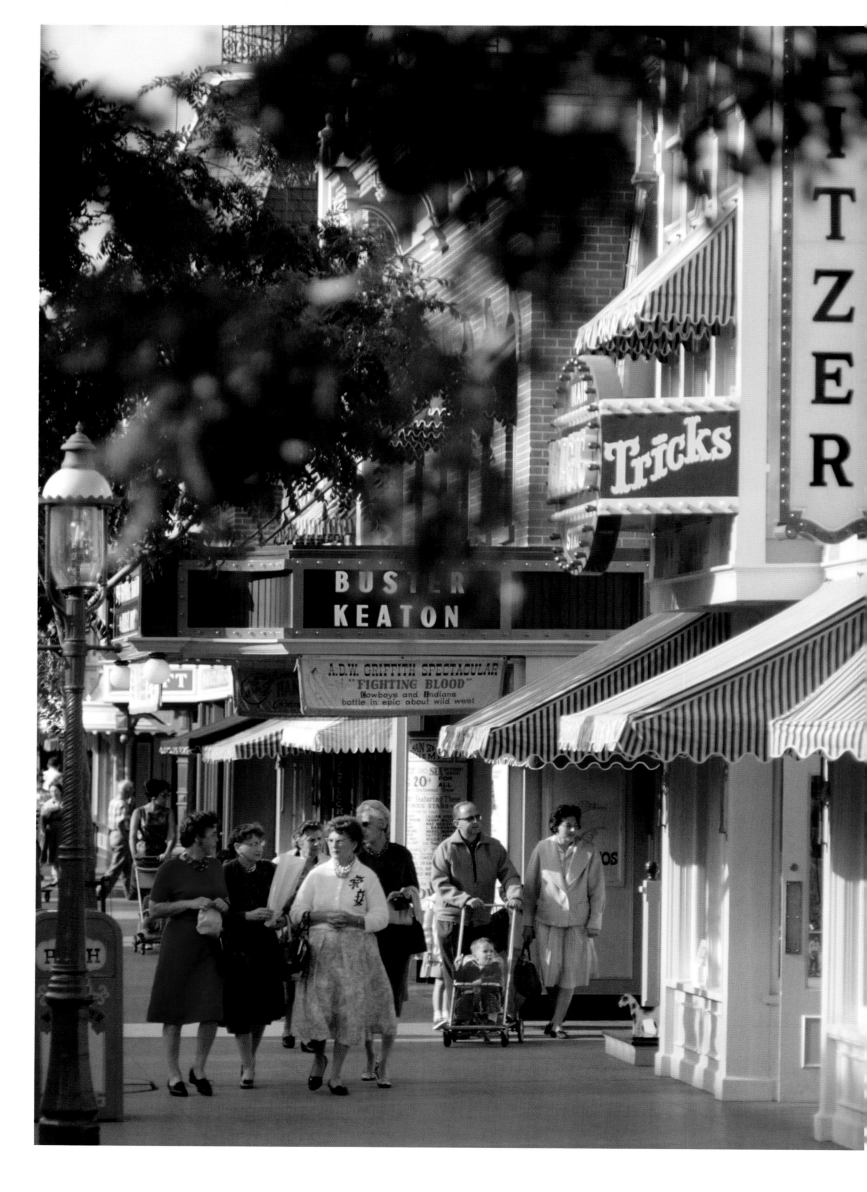

won't believe in the story. If one detail contradicts another, guests will feel let down or even deceived."[15]

Walt's meticulous attention to period detail did not extend to the unpleasant. Visual distractions make a city more vibrant, what architect Robert Venturi calls a "messy vitality," but Walt wanted to create an immersive environment that told a story. In order to avoid a cacophony of visual cues, carefully chosen architectural design elements, interiors, decor, graphic design, typeface, and colors recalled what architect Welton Becket dubbed "Total Design." The clear storytelling of an environment that is art directed to be both authentic and idealized is visually calming, emotionally directive, and effectively creates the feeling of stepping into another world.

What cast members wore played an essential part in that design, whether their characters were circa-1900 shopkeepers or drivers of horse-drawn trolleys. "We wanted them to be costumed as though they were actors in a film," remembered Hench. "They would be living in the story environment."[16] Although it was important to contribute to the authentic experience, he explained that sometimes it was more important for the costume to aid a storyline. At the Market House, for instance, the store clerks' attire was historically inaccurate: "Authentic turn-of-the-century costumes for such a place would have been mainly grey and white, but this would not be appropriate for the attraction's cheerful mood, so we opted for colorful costumes instead."[17]

Like many things in Disneyland, Main Street, U.S.A. is built at a reduced scale to create a more intimate atmosphere. Walt understood the sense of ease that came with manipulating the size of things. The desk and office that is associated with him from the TV shows was a set, Hench remembered. Walt actually worked at a child's desk. "It was a psychological ploy: When people were angry, they felt like they were towering over me," Walt confided, "and when they were asking for something, they felt more comfortable."[18] The ground floor of the shops on Main Street are built at 90 percent scale, the second floor at 80 percent, and the third even smaller. The tallest spires atop Sleeping Beauty Castle rise 77 feet (about 24 m) but appear taller because the stones at the base are larger than those near the top.

When evangelist Billy Graham dismissed Disneyland as a "nice fantasy," Walt responded, "You know the fantasy

Bank of America's Disneyland Branch, Anaheim, California

Worth seeing...the Bank that _knows_ California

Bank of America's authentic turn-of-the-century branch in Disneyland is worth seeing! Its old-fashioned atmosphere is in marked contrast to the 580 other Bank of America branches throughout California—but in one way it's still the same. Like all Bank of America branches, the service it provides is local. This on-the-spot, local service means that to out-of-state businessmen, Bank of America can offer direct representation in more than 350 California communities—can assist you with collections and credit, sales and marketing... everything from a new plant site to a new office location. If this statewide service could help your California business, why not make it a point to get in touch with us, soon?

With resources of more than nine billion dollars, Bank of America is the world's largest bank. It is owned by more than 200,000 stockholders.

Bank of America
NATIONAL TRUST AND SAVINGS ASSOCIATION
HEAD OFFICES: SAN FRANCISCO, LOS ANGELES
MEMBER FEDERAL DEPOSIT INSURANCE CORPORATION

isn't here. This is very real... The people are natural here; they're having a good time; they're communicating. This is what people really are. The fantasy is out there. Outside the gates of Disneyland, where people have hatreds and... prejudices."[19]

Let's get away from it all

The 1950s in America was a time of unprecedented peace and prosperity, and it is easy to forget how rapidly American society was changing in the postwar period, under the specter of the atomic bomb. World War I raged for four years after 1914. Liquor was outlawed from 1920 to 1933. Organized crime accompanied Prohibition, and when it was lifted, the Great Depression was in its depths. The economy picked up during World War II but families were torn apart, and the end of the war plunged the country

OPPOSITE "A surprising thing about Disney's paradise for kids is that on some days it is hard to find any bona fide children. Adults—that is, kids eighteen and over—outnumber children almost four to one. Whenever youngsters suggest going to Disneyland, their parents, uncles, aunts and grandparents always seem to join in the party."—The Saturday Evening Post, June 28, 1958. Photo, Thomas Nebbia

ABOVE Bank of America operated a working branch along Main Street. Without their $8 million line of credit, the park might have never opened.

"Main Street, U.S.A., sets the tone and pace of Disneyland: It is a place for strolling. People stop to peer into the windows of the apothecary shop and the old-time general store, and to look over the shoulder of a sidewalk artist as he sketches a portrait."

—*National Geographic, 1963*

ABOVE The Opera House was the first structure built in Disneyland. Today it is home to Great Moments with Mr. Lincoln, a show starring the "Great Emancipator" who is brought to life by *Audio-Animatronics* technology. Actor Royal Dano, who had portrayed the president on ABC's *The Rifleman* and the Emmy Award–winning series *Omnibus*, provided Lincoln's voice. *Art, Herb Ryman*

RIGHT Mickey and Minnie Mouse have always appeared in the different Disneyland parades. Just as the park has evolved over the decades, so have their features and costumes.

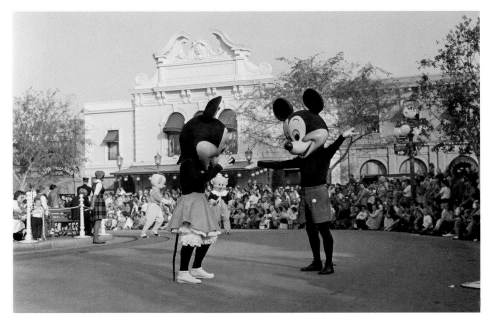

ABOVE Since its early years, Disneyland has endeavored to provide a magical experience to kids of all ages and abilities. In 1958, *The Saturday Evening Post* reported how kids from a school for the blind drove on Autopia, steered the Mark Twain Riverboat, and rode a burro through the Painted Desert. One of the children remarked, "I'll bet I have more fun than some sighted children. After all, how many kids get to steer the Mark Twain?" *Photo, Sid Avery*

OPPOSITE Each of the lands was represented in the opening day parade. Spaceman K-7 and a fleet of Autopia cars — one driven by Imagineer Bob Gurr with actor Don DeFore (who would later open the Silver Banjo restaurant in Frontierland in 1957) — cruised down Main Street for Tomorrowland. *Photo, Loomis Dean*

into the fear of communism and nuclear annihilation. The culture of fear during the 1950s was typified by science fiction and horror artistically depicting the human potential for evil and societal breakdown.

So, is it any wonder Walt begins his story of Disneyland with a walk through the last stable time period in America to restart the narrative? He asks us to look to our past to become grounded, look to our future to provide hope, look to other cultures to become part of the world we are afraid of, and look to our stories to see the potential of growth through adversity and strength in everyday life.

The shops on Main Street were similar to those found in any small town. Most sold items like fancy glassware or strawberry jam instead of Mickey Mouse T-shirts. Gibson Greeting cards sponsored the opening-day, ABC-televised invitational preview. They used their shop in the park to preview a new technology, the new Gibson "Musicards," which featured Rosemary Clooney singing "Happy Birthday." Swift's featured an old-fashioned potbellied stove and butchers in straw hats and cuffs, and originally provided all of the meat products used in the park.[20] Bank of America offered souvenir money orders at their 1900s-style bank branch.

Performers such as the Dapper Dans strolled down Main Street entertaining visitors, as did the parades that started the day the park opened. A special Holiday Festival featuring a Christmas choir event started that first year, too, evolving into what is today called the Candlelight Processional & Ceremony. Other entertainments on Main Street included the Penny Arcade, filled with pre-cinematic gadgets like the Mutoscope, which displayed a series of photographs rotated quickly enough to give the illusion of motion.

The Pavilion was an elegant restaurant with seating overlooking the Jungle Cruise, or guests could choose the "Delmonico style" wood-paneled Red Wagon Inn steakhouse across the street. Maxwell House opened a coffeehouse in Town Square, and desserts could be picked up at the Candy Palace that started offering handmade sweets by summer's end.

The Carnation Ice Cream Parlor had a soda fountain, a feature that Walt loved so much he even had one in his own home. "He had every kind of syrup and topping," Ward Kimball said. "He would fix these huge goofy things for his guests, ice cream sodas and the biggest banana split you ever saw."[21] Highlighting the soda fountain in a turn-of-the-century town was historically accurate. American ice cream parlors had hit their stride as reliable technology for creating fizzy drinks became available to entrepreneurs. By the 1950s most soda was sold in bottles, and fountains became teenage hangouts before slowly fading away.

In my merry Oldsmobile

In the months leading up to opening day, Walt sent Roger Broggie and Bob Gurr on an expedition to find antique vehicles for Main Street. "It was an all-day tour of dusty, old barns and chicken coops," Gurr remembered, "filled with hundreds of unrestored old cars and motorcycles." It was soon discovered that antiques couldn't withstand daily duty at Disneyland, so new cars had to be manufactured. "Roger told me to engineer something practical," Gurr continued. "I had a book called Floyd Clymer's *Treasury of Early Automobiles* for reference, and the studio machine shop had copies of current automotive-industry specification books. Thus started the engineering of Disneyland Main Street Vehicles, all new, but looking old."[22]

Gurr was responsible for designing a custom ice cream truck for Carnation, as well as the Omnibus, which was created with rail-car designer Eddie Sergeant, based on a 1920s double-decker bus at Travel Town in Griffith Park. At the fire station, guests could visit the horse-drawn fire wagon, which operated until 1960. Gurr was especially fond of the car he designed for Walt's personal use, an electric runabout inspired by the 1900 Oldsmobile:

We could make every visible detail authentic. We completed the runabouts with fringed surrey tops, diamond tufted seats, and special brass headlights. I developed four separate coordinated color schemes for the body paint, striping, and upholstery. Walt got his picture taken in the electric runabout with dozens of presidents, kings, and notables.[23]

But Walt's car wasn't the most impressive vehicle on Main Street. The steam-powered *C.K. Holliday*, a 5/8 scale replica of an 1869 Santa Fe locomotive, traveled a little over a mile at 20 miles per hour (about 32 km) and pulled three cattle cars, two gondola cars, and a little red caboose. It was visible everywhere in the park — the one vehicle that even the berm couldn't hide.

LEFT Visitors to the Upjohn Pharmacy exhibit experienced the sights, sounds, and smells of a 19th century apothecary shop. The elaborate exhibit included historical nebulizers, atomizers, and a glass jar filled with live leeches!

BELOW On opening day, the Eastman Kodak camera shop was one of the sponsored stores on Main Street, along with Timex next door. The watch company found an antique street clock in New York and refurbished it at its Connecticut factory before shipping it to Main Street, U.S.A. *Art, Sam McKim*

OPPOSITE Set between a shop selling jams and jellies and a coin-operated penny arcade, the Puffin Bake Shop added to the real-life turn-of-the-century ambiance of Main Street, U.S.A.

"The greatest piece of urban design in the United States today is Disneyland."

—James Rouse, Harvard University, 1963

"*Walt knew that if details are missing or incorrect, you won't believe in the story. If one detail contradicts another, guests will feel let down or even deceived.*"
—John Hench

OPPOSITE Contestants in the Disneyland pancake races had to toss a flapjack over a high ribbon and catch it in their pan four times as they ran more than 400 yards (about 370 m) down Main Street, U.S.A. The tradition, inspired by the English festivities around Shrovetide, began in 1957.

RIGHT Actress Kathleen Case had starred in several TV westerns when she was invited to the opening day festivities in Frontierland. She met the organ grinder's monkey in front of the Emporium. *Photo, Earl Leaf*

BELOW Guests dressed to the nines on opening day, enjoying popcorn from one of the many carts in the park. Today each cart is themed to its area and customized with such details as cart design and colors, signage, and Toastie-Roasties—miniature characters in each machine endlessly rotating a cylinder of popcorn. *Photo, Loomis Dean*

LEFT The "Mouse Head" balloon had been a carnival favorite since at least the 1940s. It takes a special technique to inflate them correctly. Vendors sold twice as many balloons at the west gate as the east.

BELOW A regiment of toy soldiers made their way into the Main Street Christmas parade soon after they were seen in the 1961 film *Babes in Toyland*. Photo, Bertrand Laforet

"Walt wanted the guests to enter this land under hypnosis.... A magical place where they could not see anything of the outside world."

—Herb Ryman

ABOVE "I wanted something alive, something that could grow, something I could keep plussing with ideas," Walt said of Disneyland, which he would visit a few days a week. "Not only can I add things, but even the trees will keep growing; the things will get more beautiful each year." *Photo, Thomas Nebbia*

LEFT Walt dances to a big band at the Carnation Plaza Gardens on Polka Night at the park, during the summer of 1958. The tradition lives on today with The Royal Swing Big Band Ball.

BELOW Bandleader Benny Goodman was among the famous names to play Disneyland's popular "Date Nites" held Friday and Saturday nights at the Gardens. *Photo, Lawrence Schiller*

OPPOSITE The Penny Arcade opened within the Candy Palace in 1955 and is filled with coin-operated entertainment, such as Mutoscopes, Cal-o-Scopes, and the popular Fortune Teller Esmeralda, who continues to present fortunes daily.

"*Disneyland is a place [where] you can't get lost or tired unless you want to.*"

—Walt Disney

ABOVE Bright seasonal flowers, like these pink phlox, appear in Mickey Mouse's smiling face at the park's entrance per landscape architect Ruth Shellhorn's request. Shellhorn designed many elements of the park, including the courtyard of Sleeping Beauty Castle. *Photo, Loomis Dean*

OPPOSITE On a warm Southern California day, visitors could cool down with ice cream bars from a nearby cart, or go for a classic sundae at Carnation Café or The Golden Horseshoe.

FOLLOWING Guests to Main Street, U.S.A., take their pick of public transportation to take them back in time: a roofless jitney, open-air omnibus, or a horse-drawn streetcar. Each horse receives special training to cope with the large crowds, constant noise, and other unique stimuli of Disneyland: from rolling trashcans and screaming children to stray balloons and nightly fireworks.

Adventureland

The "wonderworld" of nature's own design

The Mysterious Island, King Solomon's Mines: Mythic tales of epic journeys to undiscovered lands from the Victorian era were still essential reading by the 1950s when Walt embarked upon his plans for Adventureland. "Many of us dream of traveling to these mysterious, far-off regions of the world," he told a group of educators in 1954. "To celebrate a land that would make this dream a reality, we pictured ourselves far from civilization in the remote jungles of Asia and Africa."[1]

Walt had studied nearly every issue of *National Geographic*, looking at pictures from all over the world. Like the magazine, Walt wanted visitors to experience something beyond their front yards. Koneta Roxby, who worked in the studio research library while Disneyland was first being designed, remembered, "This library was a madhouse. There would be ten or fifteen people waiting in line for research materials and, of course, the phone rang every minute."[2]

Walt was keenly attuned to the art of bringing "exotic" locales to an audience. Hollywood had been doing this for decades with films like *Tarzan* (1936), whose tropical forest and lake were supplied by the Los Angeles County Arboretum (then the estate of Elias Jackson "Lucky" Baldwin), and *Lost Horizon* (1937), whose rugged landscape was provided by the Santa Monica Mountains.

He himself had been making nature documentaries since 1948, starting with *Seal Island*, the first film in his *True-Life Adventures* series. His brother Roy had been pessimistic about the initial reaction from distributors and theater chains: "They all say, 'Who wants to watch seals playing on a bare rock?'"[3] But *Seal Island*'s romance of discovery, coupled with its appreciation of the natural world and wildlife, won Walt his first documentary Academy Award and formed the foundation for Adventureland. He expressed his deeper motivations to a group of educators in 1953:

> *This ferment and turmoil and mystery of the world around us — exist eternally in field and wood, in desert and mountain glen, in river and on seashore, day and night, in the cycle of the seasons.... Despite their countless numbers, few people ever glimpse more than the commonest breeds of bird and beast. Nature — if we may speak of her as a universal intelligence —jealously guards her secret activities... the earth and its multitude of animal wayfarers...have helped define our culture, our arts, our behaviorism, and indeed, the fundaments of our human civilization.*[4]

A tropical oasis

Guests who stepped through the bamboo gates to Adventureland were suddenly in the midst of a distant settlement, and could choose to dine on a patio that overlooked the jungle foliage and island decor, savor tropical drinks at the Cantina, or shop at an outdoor bazaar for native handicrafts from around the world including Guatemalan textiles, Hawaiian shirts and dresses, samovars, carved elephants, jewelry, and bright-hued

OPPOSITE **Imagineer Leota Toombs was a Disney animator before joining WED Enterprises in 1962. She worked on designs for Walt Disney's Enchanted Tiki Room, Great Moments with Mr. Lincoln, and Pirates of the Caribbean, and, to this day, appears as Madame Leota, the talking head in the crystal ball at the Haunted Mansion.** *Photo, Thomas Nebbia*

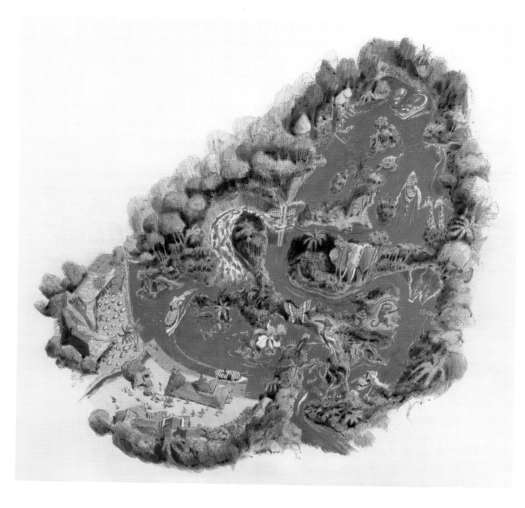

ABOVE An early plan from 1953 for the Jungle Cruise shows the extensive landscape needed for the attraction. Imagineer and horticulturist Bill Evans was in charge of securing all the tall trees and exotic — or exotic-looking — plants to create the immersive river environment. One of his tricks was to plant orange trees upside down to resemble mangroves. *Art, Harper Goff*

OPPOSITE From miniatures to full-size mock-ups, models of every part of a Disneyland attraction were integral to the design process. Walt even took them on TV. "As many as 10,000 people a day," Walt told the Disneyland audience, "have taken this boat trip safely and comfortably through the waterways of our man-made jungle."

shells. Designed by Harper Goff, it was a seductive reflection of the tropical ornamentation booming in postwar Southern California — from such restaurants as Trader Vic's and Don the Beachcomber, which established the Polynesian pop style, to Oceanic Arts in nearby Whittier, which carved and exported tiki carvings to locations around the world — including Adventureland.

Goff worked closely with landscaper Bill Evans and art director Victor Greene to procure enough mature plants for the Jungle Cruise's tropical setting and to get in a full growing season before the park even opened. Evans knew the head of the California Department of Transportation landscape architecture division, who arranged for Disneyland to receive mature palms when they were removed for construction of the Santa Ana freeway. To make sure they had enough big trees, Evans and Goff drove around older neighborhoods offering to purchase mature trees from homeowners. One very large and hard-to-find banyan tree came from an estate in Beverly Hills. Evans simulated mangroves by planting salvaged orange trees upside down, their roots reaching skyward. After a single year the jungle had filled in to the point that technicians had to carry machetes to cut through the undergrowth in order to service the equipment.

During construction, Walt drove his sponsor-provided Nash Rambler through the river channel among the newly planted trees for TV viewers of *Disneyland* to see, conjuring up the unfamiliar and vibrant sights explorers might glimpse from their boats. Even though *Audio-Animatronics* technology would not officially arrive at Disneyland until the opening of Walt Disney's Enchanted Tiki Room in 1963, the Jungle Cruise was swarming with mechanical animals that were programed with magnetic tape to move and vocalize from opening day. Bob Gurr also used such "goofy mechanical tricks" as attaching some of the animals to an aluminum casting rigged with old auto parts. "This kind of stuff is real cheap, strong, and lasts forever," he explained, "just like an old truck in the jungle."[5]

To make the sounds of wildlife and insects — such as birds singing, crickets chirping, and monkeys chattering — seem to move naturally through the trees as the boats passed, WED used self-reversing tape players that sequentially fed sound to groups of loudspeakers hidden along the route. The most complex sound effects start and stop on cue, accompanying the motion of the animals as they would in a film. James Hervey of the Los Angeles–based Ralke Company, contractors for all audiovisual effects at Disneyland, created a specialized piece of equipment called a continuous automatic fader to accomplish this amazing feat. When a boat passes a sensor, relays inside the animals are set in motion and, simultaneously, the respective animal sound is heard through a camouflaged speaker.[6]

By 1962, the Jungle Cruise attraction added nearly two dozen life-size, animated Indian elephants that frolicked in their own bathing pool, while Adventureland itself grew to include a restaurant complex, and an enormous steel-framed tree with 300,000 handmade green vinyl leaves. Inspired by the 1960 film and Johann Wyss's novel *Swiss Family Robinson*, the 80-foot (24m) man-made tree used 110 cubic yards (84 cu) of concrete, and weighed almost 150 tons (136 mt). Visitors could retrace the steps of the shipwrecked family with props from the movie as the "Swisskapolka" played in the background.

The *Safari Shooting Gallery* arrived in Adventureland in 1962, the same year the Main Street *Shooting Gallery* closed. The 12-gun range had a larger variety of targets — designed by Sam McKim — than any other gallery in the United States. Two million lead pellets were used annually between the Safari and the 1957 Frontierland *Shooting Gallery*. The pellets were so abrasive on the hand-painted backgrounds that they received a new paint job every morning, which required almost 40 gallons (150 ltr) of paint weekly. Eight times a year the surfaces had to be burned clean and completely repainted. "The painters have to be artists as well as good brush and roller men," reported the paint shop supervisor. "Several of the targets have intricate patterns like bark on the trees and spots on the giraffes. The fellows have to make them look real."[7]

Designer Rolly Crump remodeled the Adventureland Bazaar in 1961, right after WED moved to Glendale. "You carry everything with you, story wise and layout wise," the former animator remembered. "All those things you learned in animation went with you when you came to WED."[8] He took a trip to the Disneyland boneyard, where items from old attractions were stored, looking for usable scrap. Discarded ticket booths were reimagined as Moroccan tents for the cashiers. Exterior columns from the Plantation restaurant framed changing rooms for shoppers. Crump changed, customized, and painted the castoffs to create a bizarre new bazaar that also included infinity mirrors. All his hard work paid off when the boss arrived:

> Walt…said, 'Rolly you did great.' He pointed toward one of the mirrors and said [to his wife, Lillian] 'Look at the shop, it really goes on, and on, and on.' She kind of looked at him and laughed. He was like a little kid at times.[9]

Where the birds sing words and the flowers croon

Just steps away from the Main Street Central Plaza, Walt Disney's Enchanted Tiki Room stood apart as Adventureland's most technically advanced attraction at the time. The "tropical hideaway" opened in 1963 as the first *Audio-Animatronics* attraction. John Hench designed the space, originally imagined as a Polynesian restaurant as a cross-shaped room with four wings for seated dining and a central open space for the show. He made "a beautiful drawing with all these birds sitting over the tables in their cages, chirping down to people eating," recalled Crump. "Walt turned to John and said, 'We can't have birds in there…they will poop on the food.'"[10] Hench knew how to reassure Walt; they would be realistic-looking mechanical birds—that sang songs.

The computerized robotic system, which would eventually synchronize voices, music, and sound effects with the birds' movements, was a go, but the storyline wasn't clear. Enter Robert B. and Richard M. Sherman. The Sherman Brothers were Walt's in-house songwriting team. Richard shared the moment Walt approached them with the challenge:

> Walt used to bring VIPs and friends to this little tropical room in the corner of a soundstage at the studio. He'd sit them in folding chairs and down would come this cascade of flowers and birds singing songs and tikis chanting and they would look and say, "It's great but what the devil is it?" After lunch [Walt came] down to this soundstage [and said], 'you fellas are going to write me a song that'll explain all this.' So Bob and I write the song called the 'The Tiki Tiki Tiki Room' and the opening line explained everything.[11]

> ## "If I was ever going to have my park, here, at last, was a way to tell millions of people about it — with TV."
>
> **—Walt Disney**

> ## "You carry everything with you story wise and layout wise. All those things you learned in animation went with you when you came to WED."
>
> — Rolly Crump

ABOVE Postcards depicting the opening to each land were made in anticipation of the park's opening. Disney's Academy Award–winning nature documentaries, *True-Life Adventures*, which celebrated the exploration of uncharted territories and the wildlife therein, inspired the original Jungle Cruise and Adventureland itself.

OPPOSITE Walt Disney goes behind-the-scenes with writer James Cerruti (right), on assignment for the *National Geographic* cover story published in August 1963. Designers allowed the imported foliage of the Jungle Cruise enough time for a full growing season before the park opened. Soon, technicians had to carry machetes to cut through the undergrowth in order to service the equipment. *Photo, Thomas Nebbia*

FOLLOWING A baby pachyderm leaves Disneyland's backstage staff shop in 1963. Here, plaster and plastics were finished before heading to the elephant bathing pool in Adventureland, one of the many playful touches animator and Imagineer Marc Davis added to the Jungle Cruise in the 1960s. Considered one of Disney's legendary artists, he was also responsible for designing famous animated villains Cruella De Vil and Maleficent. *Photo, Thomas Nebbia*

The room where guests "all warble like nightingales" and "tikis play the drums" was quickly changed from a restaurant to an attraction when it became clear that the show was so dynamic that no diner would ever choose to leave.

Waiting visitors assembled in a forecourt for a preshow. Walt assigned the design for this area to Crump who came across the book *Voices on the Wind: Polynesian Myths and Chants* written by missionary Katharine Luomala. He used this resource for his sketches of the gods, many of which were grounded on traditional island stories like that of Tangaroa, the Māori god of the sea from which all things were created, who proudly says "from my limbs let new life fall."

But a few of the concepts were just interesting ideas Crump was toying with. When Hench showed Crump's drawings to Walt, he "looked at the one without a name and asked, "What does this one do?" Hench responded quickly: "'It's the god of tapa cloth beating.' Walt just kind of looked at it and said 'Clock?' Not missing a beat, John [Hench] shook his head [in agreement] and said, 'It's the guy that tells the time.'"[12] Walt approved it, and the Māori trickster god Maui suddenly became the keeper of "Tropic Standard Time."

With head sculptor Blaine Gibson unavailable, Crump had to learn how to sculpt in the WED parking lot, which was hot enough to keep Plasticine malleable. "You know what I sculpted with? A plastic fork! One I got right out of the studio cafeteria," he remembered.[13]

The preshow tikis were captivating, but the show inside had to be spectacular. Walt wanted 100 birds for the mobile that lowered from the ceiling above Hench's fountain in the center of the room, but Crump had to cut it down to 30 to fit in the hidden mechanical equipment. He "put a little bit of Las Vegas on those girls,"[14] dressing some of them in sequins. He also added sparkling reflectors to the eyes of the drummers so the vibrations of the drum would make them twinkle during the rainstorm, an effect created by Yale Gracey with thin strips of Mylar hidden behind bamboo. When Imagineers attempted to replicate a rainstorm using real water at Walt Disney World in Florida nearly a decade later, they discovered it didn't look as good as the Mylar, so they replaced their rain-making system with the original technique used at Disneyland.

Guests have continued to love Walt Disney's Enchanted Tiki Room and its cast of 225 birds, singing flowers, and chanting tiki gods. The iconic attraction was restored as part of the 50th anniversary of Disneyland in 2005, and is still a magnificent production. As the Sherman Brothers song says, "Most little birdies will fly away, but the Tiki Room birds are here every day."

"There was some discussion among the passengers about the animals. Were they real? (They were, of course, animated.) But in Disneyland, it is sometimes hard to know where fantasy ends and reality begins."

— *National Geographic, 1963*

OPPOSITE AND BELOW Each animal's movements are carefully thought out before they are added to the attraction. The Indian elephant wading pool was added in 1962. *Art, Marc Davis*

RIGHT The rare experience of seeing the "backside of water" while the riverboat meanders under the Schweitzer Falls is a highlight of the Jungle Cruise, consistent with Walt's goal to create the "wonder world of nature's own realm." *Art, Collin Campbell*

FOLLOWING Elephants young and old play starring roles in the Jungle Cruise in 1964 as engineers test the animatronics. When heavier elephants need some extra care and polishing, helicopters have been called in to transport them to a nearby lot. *Photo, Lawrence Schiller*

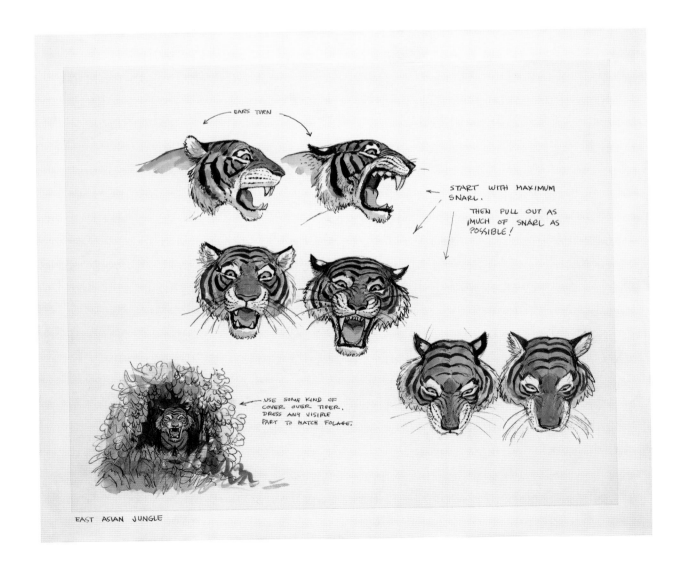

"After lunch [Walt came] down to this soundstage [and said], 'You fellas are going to write me a song that'll explain all this.'"
—**Richard M. Sherman**

INANIMATE STATUES COME
TO LIFE, BEATING THEIR DRUMS
AS THE WAR CHANT REACHES
A FRENZIED CLIMAX.

OPPOSITE The stories in the 1955 book
*Voices on the Wind: Polynesian Myths
and Chants* by missionary Katharine
Luomala served as inspiration for
the gods in the forecourt of Walt
Disney's Enchanted Tiki Room. *Art,
Rolly Crump*

ABOVE The attraction opened in
1963 with awe-inspiring *Audio-
Animatronics* and was an instant hit.
Art, Herb Ryman

RIGHT The Enchanted Tiki Room
features more than 225 *Audio-
Animatronics* performers, including
drumming tiki statues and singing
flowers. *Art, Collin Campbell*

ABOVE When Walt first saw John Hench's 1962 bird-filled Tiki Room designs (at the time it was still envisioned as a restaurant), he argued against having them: "They will poop on the food." Hench reassured Walt that they would not be live birds. *Art, John Hench*

OPPOSITE ABOVE At the Adventureland Bazaar, guests could shop for gifts from all over the world, as well as souvenirs from their favorite attractions, such as a colorful Tiki Room–inspired tray.

OPPOSITE BELOW Two years after the film *Swiss Family Robinson* was released, the *Swiss Family Treehouse* debuted in Disneyland in 1962, decorated with props used by the castaways in the film. Walt dubbed the new tree species of steel and concrete *Disneydendron Giganteum*. The 80-foot-high attraction was reimagined as Tarzan's Treehouse in 1999.

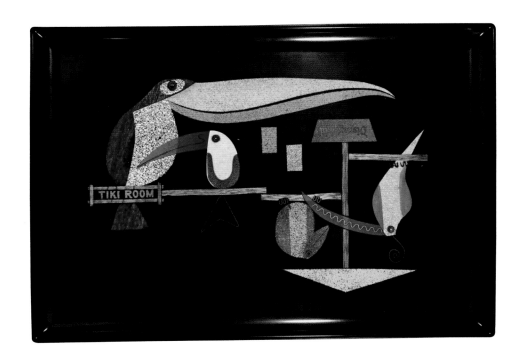

ABOVE AND OPPOSITE **Artist Paul Hartley designed many fanciful Disneyland attraction posters during the '50s and '60s, including ones for Fantasyland's Matterhorn Bobsleds, Tomorrowland's Monorail, and these proposed concepts for the Tiki Room.** *Art, Paul Hartley (opposite)*

RIGHT **"The Tiki, Tiki, Tiki Room," "Let's All Sing Like the Birdies Sing," and "The Hawaiian War Chant" make up the medley of songs the colorful, tropical cast of characters sing. Walt called on songwriting brothers Robert B. and Richard M. Sherman to write the Tiki Room song to explain the experience: "In the Tiki Room...all the birds sing words and the flowers croon."** *Art, Marc Davis*

ENCHANTED
TIKI ROOM

BIRD SINGS
ONE DEEP NOTE
(PIPE ORGAN NOTE)
BODY VIBRATES
AND CONTINUES TO
VIBRATE AFTER BEAK
CLOSES

ABOVE Marc Davis's eccentric details for the Tiki Room are amusing, but the microscopic details of the birds' movements could be easily missed and are essential to the mechanics—a testament to just how much animatronics depends on a strong animation background. *Art, Marc Davis*

LEFT Imagineers Harriet Burns, Leota Toombs, and Glendra von Kessel ready the performers for the opening night of Walt Disney's Enchanted Tiki Room. Burns was the first female Imagineer and did fine in the male-dominated environment. "She had to be as good as the men were with a table saw, lathes, drill presses... and she was," remembered Imagineer Marty Sklar, "even holding her own when the off-color jokes came her way."

BELOW The engineering side of Imagineering in 1964: The complexity of early *Audio-Animatronics* rivals that of other Space Age miracles like the jet, the laser, and the music synthesizer. "The new systems, the new devices, the new techniques which have been found feasible during years of investigation," said Disney president Donn Tatum in 1971, "will provide a body of knowledge and experience as we move into... EPCOT." *Photo, Lawrence Schiller*

FOLLOWING A musical paradise from the moment guests step into the garden filled with singing island gods, Walt Disney's Enchanted Tiki Room is a 15-minute feast for the eyes and ears that has made it one of the most popular tropical destinations. *Photo, Lawrence Schiller*

Frontierland

The ideals, the dreams, and the hard facts that have created America

The stockade gates of Frontierland stand as a symbol of military might, erected to protect a fledgling settlement in America's Old West. Endless films and novels stationed their heroes at forts, acting as pioneers defending an expanding homeland. John Wayne and Gary Cooper popularized the rough-and-tumble movie heroes on horseback, and Westerns of the 1930s and '40s inspired an endless stream of TV cowboys in the following decade: Hopalong Cassidy, the Lone Ranger, and, in a Californa twist, Walt's own masked adventurer, Zorro.

Old West fever peaked during the construction of Disneyland—no doubt shaping some of Walt's plans. The celebration of the brave frontiersman was the predominant theme, and the "King of the Wild Frontier" was Davy Crockett. Fess Parker portrayed the 19th-century folk hero in five episodes of the *Disneyland* TV show. An avalanche of Crockett merchandise, including $300 million worth of coonskin caps,[1] flew off the shelves, and Bill Hayes's rendition of the "The Ballad of Davy Crockett" topped the charts for five weeks in 1955. Three days before Disneyland opened, Walt brought Parker and costar Buddy Ebsen to a Hollywood Bowl packed with thousands of ecstatic fans. "The celestial rafters rang, and the kids rose up to roar their greeting," Cecil Smith wrote in the *Los Angeles Times*. "This was their night. And these were their heroes. And they let the grown-up world know it."[2]

In Frontierland, Walt brought history to life: Guests interacted with United States Cavalry soldiers, vaqueros from old California, and Native Americans representing 17 tribes. Walt believed in learning from the past, but the lessons still had to be entertaining. He selected a veteran of the Western movie genre to capture the United States' period of expansion and conflict, George Patrick, who had just completed art direction on two 1954 Westerns at 20th Century Fox: *The Siege at Red River* and *The Raid*. Frontiersmen wearing buckskin and fringe also met guests as they moseyed along the wooden-plank sidewalks, while desperados and heroes would leap from buildings and brawl in the streets. According to Marty Sklar of WED Enterprises, on one trip, King Mohammed V of Morocco was caught off guard by the authenticity of the performances:

> Although the park worked closely with State Department security for all these visits…somehow the "Western bad man"…did not get the word about the head of state's visit. When "Black Bart" started to go into his act, and reached for the gun in his holster, he realized just in time that there were at least half a dozen weapons pointed at him—and none of them had blanks.[3]

In the area outside the Davy Crockett Frontier Museum, the U.S. Marshal's Office, jail, assay office, and general store, guests could watch horses being shod at the blacksmith shop and harnesses being made

FRONTIER LAND

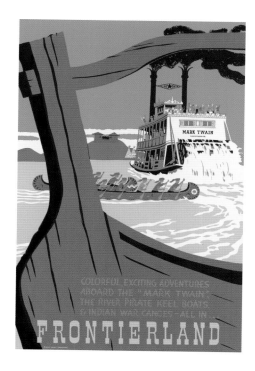

next door.[4] Or they could stop at the Davy Crockett Frontier Arcade to fire an authentic Western "buffalo gun." Or take a buckboard to the Pendleton Woolen Mills to buy an Indian trade blanket or a plaid shirt, then climb aboard a stagecoach to tour the Painted Desert.

The best show in Frontierland, however, wasn't on the streets; it was in The Golden Horseshoe saloon. When Walt asked Harper Goff to replicate the saloon from *Calamity Jane* (1953), he had no idea that Goff designed that set for the movie. The designer dusted off his blueprints of the set and asked fellow designer Stan Jolley to help flesh out the interior. Walt had a reserved box next to the stage and auditioned the original cast of The Golden Horseshoe Revue, which featured Judy Marsh as Slue Foot Sue (Betty Taylor took over the role from 1956–1987) and Wally Boag as Pecos Bill, along with plenty of can-can dancers. Opening-day advertising promised that in addition to a rollicking stage show, guests sidling up to the counter would be surrounded by "all the familiar Wild West characters: the traders and trappers, cow hands, 'two-gun' men, dudes, and dancehall girls."[5]

Frontierland was wide open, and also featured an Indian trading post,[6] a New Orleans area, and the restaurant Casa de Fritos, with its "atmosphere of authentic Old Mexico." Guests could join "the hardy pioneers to blaze new trails in the Golden

West" aboard various early modes of transport, or "take a prospector's trip, packing into the desert with a burro train in search of gold and adventure."[7]

Roads, riverbeds, and railroads

Walt had a deep respect for nature and was concerned about its stewardship. His 1953 *True-Life Adventures* film, *The Living Desert*, had won an Academy Award, and he wanted to bring the grandeur of the Southwestern landscape to Frontierland. During National Wildlife Week more than a decade later, Walt proclaimed:

> *If certain events continue, most of America's natural beauty will become nothing more than a memory. The natural beauty of America is a treasure found nowhere else in the world. Our forests, water, grasslands, and wildlife must be wisely protected and used.*[8]

The day the park opened, Frontierland was a rough sketch of its present self, a simulated wilderness crisscrossed by the trails used by mule packs, stagecoaches, and soon Conestoga wagons. There was more adventure to be had on the water. Just beyond the town crossroads, passengers could board the 105-foot (32-m) long, 150-ton (about 136-t) Mark Twain Riverboat to explore the Rivers of America. A joint project built between the Todd Shipyards in San Pedro, California, and the Disney soundstages, the riverboat was the first stern-wheeler constructed in the United States in more than 50 years. At its debut, it steamed by a riverfront built to resemble Southern towns like Mississippi's Natchez, Alabama's Mobile, and Louisiana's New Orleans. A little less than a year later, visitors could ride the rivers in the Indian War Canoes, later renamed Davy Crockett's Explorer Canoes, and in 1958, the Sailing Ship Columbia, a full-sized replica of the first ship to carry the American flag around the world from 1787 to 1790, joined the Mark Twain. The windjammer was designed from historical plans and also crafted by Todd Shipyards and the Walt Disney studios.

Back on land, a guest could take a trip to Holidayland, the "countryside of yesterday's rural America," located just outside the berm between Adventureland and Frontierland. This gay land was open to businesses and other groups for picnics and featured pony-drawn buggy and surrey rides, a bandstand, baseball diamond, and celebrations for every season, including egg-rolling contests in spring and ice carnivals in winter.

Frontierland's train station was built from the original working drawings for the Disney film about a young farm boy, *So Dear to My Heart* (1949). Whistles from the Disneyland Railroad sometimes spooked horses and eventually contributed to the end of animal-driven rides in Frontierland. The station is still in use today, and has a telegraph constantly tapping out Walt's speech from opening day.

A land of plenty

Less than a year after Disneyland opened, Walt greatly expanded the desert area of Frontierland. A train ride was added through an old mining town with teetering rocks, a natural arch bridge, and a series of "underground" caverns. The glowing interiors were filled with fountains, geysers, multicolored stalactites and stalagmites, and 22 breathtaking water effects including Rainbow Falls, where water cascaded down in eight different colors that glowed under blacklight. The train was fittingly named the Rainbow Caverns Mine Train, and the stagecoach and mule pack that had been introduced on Disneyland's opening day were renamed the Rainbow Mountain Stage Coaches and Rainbow Ridge Pack Mules.

The Indian Village, which presented the authentic dances of different Native American tribes, grew significantly in 1956, and was enlarged again in 1962. Tribal members hired by the park built their own dwellings and totem poles, and created birch-bark lodges and tepees. Their day-to-day presence was groundbreaking in an era when many visitors' exposure to Native Americans was limited to those on their TV screens. At the 1958 dedication of the Grand Canyon Diorama, 96-year-old Hopi Chief Nevangnewa blessed the trains that would carry visitors past the world's longest diorama at the time, which depicted the flora and fauna of Arizona's great South Rim abyss.

Nesbitt's, the soda company, sponsored a new attraction in 1956: Tom Sawyer Island, where Walt enthusiastically told columnist Bennett Cerf, "The only way kids can get to it will be by raft!"[9] The island featured docks for fishing, trails and caves to explore, Fort Wilderness, a suspension bridge, a burning settler's cabin, and lifelike North American wildlife. Although Walt designed much of the island himself, Sam McKim created renderings for the Old Mill, Fort Wilderness,

and the tree house, and Emile Kuri found taxidermy animals for the far end of the island. Walt said of the expansion, "This is proof of our success…I wouldn't be able to get money for expansion if Disneyland hadn't been paying off."[10] The park saw two million guests during the first six months, with adults outnumbering children three to one.

A big part of that success was a constant desire to push the limits of technology. More than 200 mechanical animals, including birds, bears, beavers, and reptiles, were added to Frontierland in 1960 to augment the newly reimagined Mine Train Through Nature's Wonderland (which presented and incorporated pieces of the previous Rainbow Caverns Mine Train experience in a new way), though the native fauna of Anaheim didn't always appreciate their mechanical counterparts. "Right after the first birds were installed, a big ruckus was going on," said Bob Gurr. "Seems the real birds resented the presence of the phony birds and were pecking them to bits."[11]

Gurr explained how he and the WED Imagineers got lifelike movements without the programing that generally was involved for more sophisticated *Audio-Animatronics* figures: "The elk machine was basically two elks connected at the antlers. By adjusting the air-valve flow rates, we could get a real random but predictable action almost as good as the later fully programmable digital show control systems." He added that the elk ran "trouble-free" for many years. The talented crew at WED Enterprises could ensure that Walt's visions were realized even years before the technology caught up with them.

Walt wrote in 1958 of the Western expansion that inspired Frontierland and those who made it possible:

> All of us, whether 10th generation or naturalized Americans, have cause to be proud of our country's history, shaped by the pioneering spirit of our forefathers. It is to those hardy pioneers, men of vision, faith, and courage, that we have dedicated Frontierland.[12]

He could have very well used those same words to describe the innovators—including himself—who made Frontierland a reality.

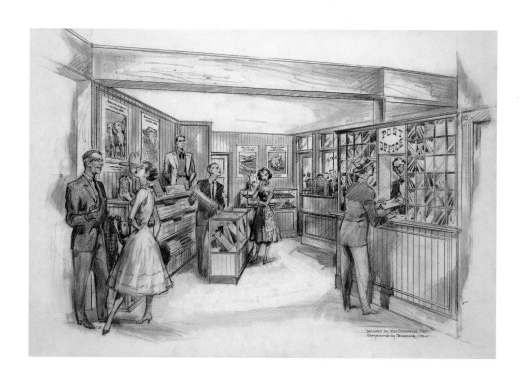

ABOVE Native American jewelry, baskets, and headdresses are offered for sale in an early rendering of a Frontierland Trading Post. Early gift shops in the Davy Crockett Frontier Arcade area included the Bonekraft store, which sold bone jewelry; and Pendleton Woolen Mills, which featured Indian trading blankets. *Art, Sam McKim*

LEFT The "World's Biggest Cowboy Buckle" was displayed in the Pendleton Woolen Mills store window on opening day at Disneyland. And that wasn't the only attraction at the store: It also featured an old-fashioned post office. *Art, Sam McKim*

OPPOSITE Stylish guests model dresses with Western-inspired images, fitting for Frontierland.

"The natural beauty of America is a treasure found nowhere else in the world. Our forests, water, grasslands, and wildlife must be wisely protected and used."

—Walt Disney

ride the MINE TRAIN thru **NATURE'S WONDERLAND**

RIVERS OF AMERICA

LIVING DESERT

OLYMPIC ELK

BEAR COUNTRY

BEAVER VALLEY

PACK MULE TRAIL

RAINBOW CAVERNS

a preview of new attractions in
DISNEYLAND '60

OPPOSITE **Fossilized remains in the desert sands of Rainbow Ridge were among the unique sites mule riders came across in 1960.** *Photo, Ralph Crane*

ABOVE **More than 200 mechanical animals—including birds, bears, beavers, and reptiles—were added to Frontierland in 1960 to expand the Mine Train, which by then traveled not only through the Rainbow Caverns, but also through Nature's Wonderland, inspired by Disney's** *True-Life Adventures* **documentaries.**

LEFT The green, black, and blue ore cars designed by Bob Gurr for the Rainbow Caverns Mine Train got a sunny paint job when more than 200 animated animals, birds and reptiles were added in 1960 for the expansion of the attraction into Natures Wonderland. When the Mine Train first opened in 1956, it traveled through the Rainbow Desert (later renamed the Living Desert when Nature's Wonderland opened in 1960), passing bubbling pots, balancing rocks, and other natural wonders of the West. The attraction closed in 1977. *Photo, Ralph Crane*

ABOVE Guests on the Mine Train were welcomed by fantasy flora like a smiling saguaro cactus.

OPPOSITE **Actor-turned-artist Sam McKim created renderings for Tom Sawyer Island's various sites: the old mill, Fort Wilderness, and the tree house, which was made of shipping crates that Tom appeared to have scavenged around the Mississippi River.** *Photo, George S. Kuntz, MD*

ABOVE **When columnist Bennett Cerf (who cofounded publishing giant Random House) visited Disneyland in early spring of 1956, Walt showed him where Tom Sawyer Island would be built, boasting, "The only way kids can get to it will be by raft!" Cerf described Disneyland in his April 15, 1956, article for** *This Week Magazine* **as "a Coney Island of the atomic age" and wrote of Walt, "Disney obviously remains a kid himself—that, I think, is the secret of his unique appeal." Here, Walt's daughter Sharon takes in a preview rendering.**

"*[In Frontierland] we meet the America of the past, out of whose strength and inspiration came the good things of life we enjoy today.*"

—Walt Disney

ABOVE An early rendering for "Disneyland" placed the Indian Settlement outside the gates of "Frontier Country." On opening day the Indian Village bordered Frontierland and Adventureland. *Art, Herb Ryman*

OPPOSITE The park hired members of 17 tribes to build their own dwellings and totem poles, and create birch-bark lodges and tepees. Although some totems were carved on site, these colorful totems from 1960 were made in the staff shop backstage at Disneyland.

FOLLOWING Guests enjoyed the regular live shows at the Indian Village, where tribal members performed authentic ceremonial dances and rituals that welcomed audience participation. *Photo, George S. Kuntz, MD*

OPPOSITE **Duels, showdowns, and chases unfolded on the streets of early Frontierland. This epic battle featured the characters from Disney's TV series** *Zorro*, **which was set during the time when California was ruled by Spain.** *Photo, Allan Grant*

ABOVE **For the Golden Horseshoe, Harper Goff replicated his saloon set from the 1953 film** *Calamity Jane*, **while fellow designer Stan Jolley fleshed out the interior. Walt had a box seat next to the stage to enjoy the revue, starring Betty Taylor as Slue-Foot Sue and Wally Boag as Pecos Bill. The** *Guinness Book of World Records* **cited it for the most performances in the history of theater when it ended on October 12, 1986.** *Photo, Loomis Dean*

FOLLOWING **Stars of hit Disney TV shows occasionally appeared at the park: Fess Parker took part in the opening-day ceremonies as Davy Crockett, and Guy Williams attracted legions of fans when he appeared as Zorro in 1958.** *Photo, Allan Grant*

Fantasyland

Timeless land of enchantment

At the heart of Disneyland is Sleeping Beauty Castle. The stone fortress that surrounds Fantasyland is the visual, thematic, and literal center of the park. Castle designer Marvin Davis said that the castle was Walt's idea: It was what he "had the most vivid picture of in his mind...Fantasyland with the entrance through a castle."[1] Many concepts were tried: a Robin Hood castle, a Cinderella palace, a fantasy building reminiscent of a castle, no castle at all. *Sleeping Beauty* (1959) was still in preproduction at Walt Disney Productions when the palace, reminiscent of Neuschwanstein Castle in Bavaria, rose up above the moat.

On opening day, an armored knight on horseback rode up to the drawbridge over the swan-filled moat and proclaimed, "Open the Fantasyland castle in the name of the children of the world!" Mickey joined the ecstatic children who ran through the entrance for the first time. Walt talked about what inspired the land:

When we were planning Fantasyland, we recalled the lyrics of the song, "When You Wish Upon a Star." The words of the melody, from our picture Pinocchio [1940], inspired us to create a land where dreams come true. What youngster, listening to parents or grandparents read aloud, does not dream of flying with Peter Pan over moonlit London, or tumbling into Alice's nonsensical Wonderland? In Fantasyland, these classic stories of everyone's youth have become realities for youngsters of all ages to participate in.[2]

Although it is Walt Disney's animated film versions of *Peter Pan, Alice in Wonderland*, or *The Wind in the Willows* we think of today, it was the original British novels that first captured Walt's fancy. The same artists who brought the stories to celluloid were often asked to recreate their fantasies in three dimensions for Disneyland.

The age of chivalry, magic, and make-believe are reborn

Cross the castle drawbridge and before you is the King Arthur Carrousel, the centerpiece of Fantasyland, complete with 72 regal steeds prancing to calliope melodies. Medieval tournament pavilions contained many happy ports of fantasy ringing the courtyard, from the Chicken of the Sea Pirate Ship and Restaurant docked by Skull Rock, to a mad tea party of enormous spinning teacups. The Casey Jr. Circus Train puffed merrily among the hills of Storybook Land and guests soared into the air on Dumbo the Flying Elephant. Visitors explored the diamond mines with Snow White and the Seven Dwarfs, took a spin with Mr. Toad in a 1903-esque jalopy, or had Welch's grape juice with the Mickey Mouse Club gang in their own tentlike theater.

Every ride in Fantasyland (except the historic 1922 carousel) was custom built, designed by WED Enterprises art directors and engineered by Arrow Development in Mountain View, California. During early design stages, Walt would view storyboards and act out the narrative. Fantasyland's lead art

OPPOSITE **The drawbridge to Sleeping Beauty Castle was lowered for the first time on opening day, and only once since: when the redesigned Fantasyland opened on May 25, 1983. The castle sits at the center of Disneyland and is one of the world's most recognizable structures, with spires that rise as high as 77 feet (about 24 m), but it wasn't the first concept Walt had in mind. A palace for Cinderella and a castle for Robin Hood were considered in the planning stages.** *Photo, Allan Grant*

director, Bill Martin, became an expert in track design. "Walt Disney looked to him for area layout. [Bill] was like an architect, art director, show writer, a jack of all trades," Bob Gurr remembered. "He would take a big plan view and make a drawing and not only visualize how everything would look, but how it would look in 3-D."[3] Other contributors included Ken Anderson, who was one of the lead designers on several Fantasyland attractions including Snow White's Adventures and Mr. Toad's Wild Ride, two of the first dark rides (indoor shows with blacklight effects). He worked with Stan Jolley, a former art director at 20th Century Fox, and Claude Coats, who had been trained as an architect and painted backgrounds both for the rides and the films that inspired them.

Lessons learned designing dark rides and innovative new vehicle systems—for Dumbo the Flying Elephant, Casey Jr.

Circus Train, and the Mad Tea Party,—culminated in the complete revolution of roller-coaster technology: the Matterhorn Bobsleds. "Imagine having to build a dark ride system," asked historian Robert Reynolds. "It had to be quiet, able to take tight turns, reliable, be simple to repair, and able to operate 14 hours a day every day."[4] Arrow Development spent more on research and development than the fixed bid they agreed to. "After it was all over, Walt Disney said, 'How did you boys come out on the rides?'" recalled Arrow's Karl Bacon. "I told him that we lost money. He said, 'I don't want you to lose any money on my work, I'll cover your costs.'"[5] And he did.

Walt's close working relationship with Arrow is epitomized in the development of their first collaboration, Mr. Toad's Wild Ride, which took inspiration from a little antique car in Karl Bacon and Ed Morgan's shop yard. WED designer Bruce Bushman made an original sketch of the vehicle, and then Arrow created a prototype, made plywood templates from the prototype, and used the templates for the sheet-metal parts. Just 12 Arrow vehicles propelled nearly 700 guests an hour through a tight weaving course that literally travels to hell and back—a testament to the meeting of WED's artistic genius and Arrow's engineering brilliance.

Gurr remembers lying on his back underneath the Mad Tea Party's spinning teacups, looking for wear and tear while the ride was running. Redesigning the teacups was a confidence builder for the group of artists turned engineers that formed the early WED Enterprises. "By 1956," Gurr says, "Walt Disney Productions became a full-fledged ride and show manufacturer."[6]

Just around the corner, Alice in Wonderland's three-wheeled vehicles, which debuted in 1958, would become the model for many of the tracked rides in the park. They curve a course of tight turns through the "upside-down" room, the court of the Queen of Hearts, and a garden of oversized flowers—a visualization of Alice's mixed-up thoughts. Gurr shared how they came into being:

> There were 10-foot-tall [about 3 m] flowers for Alice in Wonderland animated by one motor and lots of push rods. During testing, half were busted. The team got cracking. What to do? We needed a material that is light and fatigue resistant, one that can bend all day … A fishing pole! I drove down to the Sila-Flex fish-pole

company in Costa Mesa and got them to make a whole bunch of plain fishing poles with no eyelets. These things worked forever after.[7]

The anthropomorphic Casey Jr. Circus Train from *Dumbo* (1941) came to life at Disneyland, rolling around the hills of Fantasyland pulling cars painted with the names "Monkeys" and "Wild Animals." Creating a locomotive with the agility of a roller coaster tested the mechanical skills of the folks at Arrow Development. Placing the engineer up front and disguising a Plymouth engine as a calliope made it possible for the little engine to chug up hills.

For visitors entering Fantasyland from the east side, the open mouth of Monstro the Whale from *Pinocchio* beckons brave riders to find their own inner Moby Dick aboard the Storybook Land Canal Boats. Miniatures, like the ones that originally entranced Walt, lined the shore at 1:12 scale, creating a literary landscape of fairy tale homes and detailed European villages surrounded by tiny shrubs, flowers, and trees, including a century-old bonsai pine tree purportedly planted by Walt himself.

The happiest kingdom of them all

In addition to attractions, there were shows in the Fantasyland of the 1950s. Beloved by generations of Disney fans, an early version of the Mickey Mouse Club debuted in the 1930s as a movie-theater promotion. The television series of the same name premiered in 1955 and was a variety show with cartoons, dancing, and musical numbers. It was an instant hit and profits from the show helped to finance the park. On August 27, 1955, the Mickey Mouse Club Theater opened where Pinocchio's Daring Journey is today. Annette Funicello was the show's breakout star and appeared at Disneyland events along with hosts Jimmie Dodd, Roy Williams (another Disneyland addition plucked from The Walt Disney Studios), and other cast members.[8]

At the northeast of Fantasyland, a group of 80-year-old circus wagons were restored and stationed along the approach to the candy-striped Mickey Mouse Club Circus tent, home to many acts: animal trainer George Keller (who Walt thought was "amazing… I think Keller hypnotizes the beasts"[9]) and the Ted DeWayne's Troupe of acrobats, gymnasts, and a trapeze artist. Walt hoped it

ABOVE **Skyway riders enjoyed the thrilling trip through the Matterhorn above speeding bobsledders in 1963. The attraction connected Fantasyland to Tomorrowland for almost four decades before it closed in 1994.** *Photo, William Wanamaker*

would become a permanent feature, but the circus only ran two months. Once the circus was removed "Walt needed to fill the space with something quick and simple," Gurr noted. "Adding Autopia Jr. and a small river connected to Fantasyland and a small railroad (the Viewliner) was the plan."[10]

A revolutionary ride

Holiday Hill served as the original buffer between Fantasyland and Tomorrowland. This mountain of dirt excavated during construction of the castle moat featured landscaped hiking trails. One year after the park opened, a support column for the Skyway attraction was planted on top. Walt was an investor in the Sugar Bowl ski resort near Lake Tahoe and admired the gondola used to transport visitors from the highway to Mt. Disney. He brought a Swiss-made aerial tramway to Disneyland to transport guests between Fantasyland and Tomorrowland in colorful passenger buckets suspended from a 2,400-foot-long (nearly 732 m) cable. Dr. Walter Schmid, the Swiss consul general of Los Angeles, attended the dedication ceremony on June 23, 1956.

Walt wanted a proper mountain to go with his gondola, and three years later he got one, the Matterhorn, complete with mountain climbers on its opening day, June 14, 1959. The Skyway's tower determined the position and height of the Matterhorn. While filming the live-action film *Third Man on the Mountain* (1959) on location near Zermatt,

Switzerland, he started to plan an attraction that captured the excitement of sledding down the famous peak. Walt had said time and time again that he didn't want thrill rides or roller coasters in the park, and insisted that the Matterhorn Bobsleds—added as part of a large expansion the same year the film was released—had to be different.

Expert rockwork artist Fred Joerger studied photos of the Swiss mountain to create the mottled finish. He built models in the studio's styling shop, which led to blueprints and finally the 147-foot-high (about 45 m) mountain, an exact 1:100 scale replica of the actual peak. Santa Monica–based James L. Barnes Construction Company used a steel frame and enough lumber to build a residential neighborhood. Although it would be visible for miles outside the park, designers incorporated forced perspective with trees growing progressively smaller as they reach the peak so the mountain would appear even larger from below. And designing the ride inside was no small feat either, Gurr related:

> *Coaster dynamics, speed, up-and-down slopes, banking, bank change rates, variable guest weights, friction coefficient based on how long the car has been running, temperature of the day. All these had to be figured out first so I would have a menu of design criteria for the track layout.*[11]

Traditional roller-coaster tracks utilize angle iron, but the track inside the Matterhorn was tubular steel. The car sat low, and the wheels were made from Polyurethane, a new plastic developed in Germany during World War II. The exterior of the Matterhorn was designed before the roller coaster itself, and engineers struggled to fit the angles and turns needed for the bobsleds to function in such a confined space. It was the first roller coaster that allowed for multiple vehicles on the same track at once. "We had to bridge the distances between the supports they gave us," Ed remembered.[12] "We had to establish the friction slope for the ride," Karl added, and "miss the other track with proper crossover points...there was not a lot of room."[13] And it had to be designed and built in only 10 months.

Arrow Development labored over the technology needed to simulate a smooth toboggan ride down a snowy peak. The team designed side-mounted wheels and grooves in the cars to create a safe, fast, and

ABOVE **Walt drew inspiration from his favorite elements from the Griffith Park Merry-Go-Round for his King Arthur Carrousel. Arrow Engineering rebuilt an antique found in Canada into a four-row, 85-horse machine and studio artists converted all the horses into jumpers.**

OPPOSITE **A couple enjoys the first high school "Grad Nite" at Disneyland in 1961, with festivities that started at 11 P.M. and lasted until dawn, including dancing and live entertainment. Musicians from Smokey Robinson and Linda Ronstadt to the bands Berlin and No Doubt all performed at Disneyland. The tradition relocated to Disney California Adventure in 2013.** *Photo, Ralph Crane*

smooth ride. The result was revolutionary and became the standard for all modern roller coasters. Even the seating arrangement was pioneering: "I patterned the Matterhorn guest seating design after the Swiss bobsled arrangement," Gurr continued. "This allowed the folks to snuggle together—a plan that later proved delightful to young couples."[14]

Before the bobsleds opened to the public, construction boss Admiral Joe Fowler asked for a test ride on the unfinished track, which ended 60 feet (about 18 m) above the ground. To stop he had to run into sandbag after sandbag while squeezing a handbrake. He "got into a sled and we hoisted it with a big long reach crane and dropped it on the track," recalled Ed Morgan. "Joe's eyes were as big as dinner plates when he came down, but things stopped and a big grin came back on his face."[15]

Crews worked day and night to finish on time, and designer Ed Morgan wanted to be especially careful. "We didn't really get the chance to test the whole thing at one time," he remembered, "until almost hours before opening."[16] So he asked for extra redundancy and to run the cars slower. Morgan detailed his client's reaction on opening day:

Walt was upset because the lines were clear around the mountain twice. I told him my concerns and he just shook his head and shuffled off. That was it. No further conversation.... All of Hollywood was there. Walt Disney walked down the line and apologized...One thing they wouldn't do is take those people and give them special treatment ahead of everyone else.[17]

Marty Sklar remembered when King Baudouin of Belgium rode the bobsleds and inquired why the mountain "had holes in it." Walt responded, "Because it's a Swiss mountain!"[18]

The Matterhorn is so unique to Disneyland that it was never replicated in any other Disney park. And the most beloved character atop the mountain is Tinker Bell, who began setting off the "Fantasy in the Sky" fireworks show in 1961. Building the Matterhorn gave Tinker Bell a place to launch her nightly flight, helping to bring to life the iconic opening of the *Disneyland* TV show. Real life imitating art. "Fantasy, if it's really convincing, can't become dated," Walt Disney said, "for the simple reason that it represents a flight into a dimension that lies beyond the reach of time."[19]

LEFT Child star Shirley Temple, who had attended the 1937 premiere of *Snow White and the Seven Dwarfs*, dedicated the Sleeping Beauty Castle Walkthrough attraction, which opened in 1957.

BELOW Herb Ryman was instrumental in developing the final look of Sleeping Beauty Castle. He was not a fan of the original configuration of the model by Fred Joerger, so he took parts of the castle model, turned them around, and created the iconic entrance. Walt approved. *Art, Herb Ryman*

OPPOSITE It was fitting that Eyvind Earle, the production designer of the 1959 animated feature *Sleeping Beauty*, was called upon to create several tableaux for the inside of the castle. *Art, Eyvind Earle*

FOLLOWING Earle's signature color styling transported guests into the world of Sleeping Beauty by seamlessly matching the mood of the film. *Art, Eyvind Earle*

SLEEPING BEAUTY CASTLE
COMES TO
ANAHEIM JULY 1955

BIT O' SWITZERLAND...
THE MATTERHORN & SKYWAY

ABOVE The Matterhorn Bobsleds opened on June 14, 1959, at Disneyland, and have never been replicated outside of the park. Its 147-foot-tall (nearly 45 m) "mountain" was inspired by Walt Disney's visit to Switzerland during filming of *Third Man on the Mountain* in the summer of 1958. (This rendering was completed later the same year.) *Art, Sam McKim*

RIGHT Walt gave the first ride on the Swiss-built Skyway to Dr. Walter Schmid, Swiss consul general of Los Angeles, in 1956. The attraction connected Fantasyland to Tomorrowland for almost four decades before it closed in 1994.

OPPOSITE June 14, 1959, marked the grand opening of three "E" ticket attractions, a new designation for the most anticipated attractions: the Disneyland-Alweg Monorail System, Matterhorn Bobsleds, and Submarine Voyage. Costumed Swiss dancers added a festive flair to the opening ceremonies for the Matterhorn. *Photo, Ralph Crane*

ABOVE Real mountain climbers ascend the perfect 1:100 scale recreation of the famous Swiss peak at 1960. Walt had named the climbers Hans, Otto, and Fritz when the Matterhorn first opened. The climbers have retired but will occasionally return for very special events like the 50th anniversary of the park in 2005 or the launch of the revamped bobsleds in 2012. *Photo, Ralph Crane*

"*I patterned the Matterhorn guest seating design after the Swiss bobsled arrangement. This allowed the folks to snuggle together — a plan that later proved delightful to young couples.*"

—Bob Gurr

ABOVE The Matterhorn crest appears on the front of each vehicle and as an embroidered patch on the jackets and shirts of the cast members. There were various patch designs produced in just the first two years of the attraction and are popular among collectors.

RIGHT Walt rode the Matterhorn with Disneyland hostess Donna Jackson, and his special guests, the Shah of Iran and Empress Farah, on April 25, 1962, while the couple was touring Southern California.

FOLLOWING At the height of the Cold War, stars of the 1962 comedy *40 Pounds of Trouble* — actors Suzanne Pleshette, Claire Wilcox, and Tony Curtis — wear Nikita Khrushchev, Fidel Castro, and John F. Kennedy masks while hiding out at the Chicken of the Sea restaurant during filming. *Photo, Leo Fuchs*

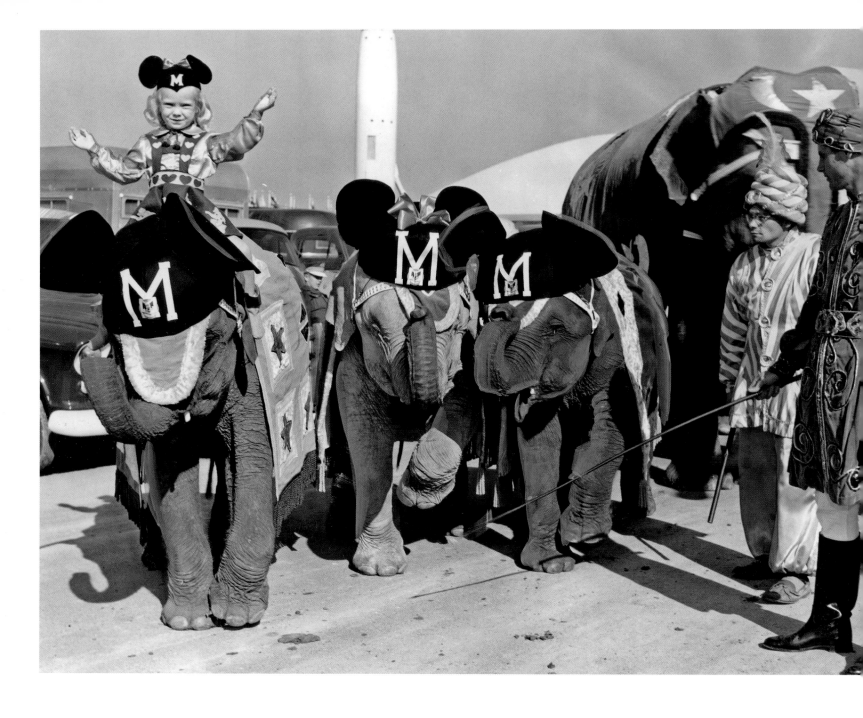

"*Fantasy, if it's really convincing,
can't become dated for the simple reason
that it represents a flight into a dimension
that lies beyond the reach of time.*"

—**Walt Disney**

OPPOSITE **Five-year-old Kandra K. Craig paraded a group of baby elephants around the park at the debut of the Mickey Mouse Club Circus on November 25, 1955.** *The Mickey Mouse Club* **star Jimmie Dodd was the ringmaster of the six-week show that featured acrobats, seals, tigers, and clowns.**

RIGHT **Large silkscreened attraction posters advertise a trio of Fantasyland opening attractions in 1955, including Dumbo the Flying Elephant, which features Disney tunes played by an organ built in 1915.** *Art, Bjorn Aronson*

BELOW **On Catholic Schools Day at Disneyland a group of nuns took their habits to new heights while riding Dumbo. The special promotional day started in 1961 and featured free prizes and discounted rates for Catholic school families and teachers.**

ABOVE Walt asked Arrow Development to incorporate elements of the Griffith Park Merry-Go-Round into his King Arthur Carrousel. Designers transformed a vintage 1922 Dentzel model with three rows of assorted animals into a four-row showstopper where every horse was a jumping steed with a jewel-encrusted harness. He wanted the centerpiece of Fantasyland to be more like his neighborhood favorite, with horses in a leaping pose. *Art, Bruce Bushman*

RIGHT The color scheme and caption of 1954 concept art for the Dumbo ride allude to the surrealist "Pink Elephants on Parade" sequence from the 1941 animated feature. *Art, Bruce Bushman*

DUMBO
"PINK ELEPHANT" RIDE
FANTASYLAND

LEFT AND BELOW Early drawings by art director and artist Bruce Bushman of the Mad Tea Party, which was inspired by a scene in the 1951 film *Alice in Wonderland*, show the different features that didn't make the final attraction—from an actual teapot to the Mad Hatter himself. Bushman's early involvement in the design of Fantasyland contributed greatly to the look and feel of the finished attractions. *Art, Bruce Bushman*

ABOVE **Engineering and construction of the spinning teacups almost proved maddening for WED Enterprises, recalled Imagineer Bob Gurr. Ultimately the revisions and redesigns that went into the ride and other Fantasyland attractions strengthened the partnership between WED Enterprises and ride developer Arrow Development.** *Photo, Loomis Dean*

"Disneyland is two years old and continues to delight ... it doesn't lose its luster in a day's visit, nor in two or three. Possibly it never will for a good many visitors."

—*Sunset*, 1957

LEFT **Goofy joined a teacup full of children for a spin in 1964. Some incarnation of the popular attraction can be found at nearly every Disneyland-style Disney park across the globe.** *Photo, Lawrence Schiller*

OPPOSITE **As they do today, roaming costumed characters in the early 1960s offered Fantasyland guests a chance to meet their favorite animated Disney stars.** *Photo, Lawrence Schiller*

ABOVE **Monstro the Whale, from** *Pinocchio*, **guards the entrance to the Storybook Land Canal Boats. His giant blinking eye and spouting blowhole sometimes surprised guests posing for photos.**

OPPOSITE **Monstro the Whale, from the 1940 animated feature** *Pinocchio*, **was first imagined as an attraction from which flat-bottomed boats plunged into a lagoon. This concept art was completed in 1954. Eventually Monstro was integrated into the Storybook Land Canal Boats.** *Art, Bruce Bushman*

RIGHT **After early design challenges hampered Canal Boats of the World, the attraction was closed and later reopened on June 16, 1956, as Storybook Land Canal Boats. The re-themed ride included scenes from Disney films, which increased its popularity.** *Art, Bruce Bushman*

OPPOSITE **King Bhumibol and Queen Sirikit of Thailand visited the park with their children in 1960, and Walt came along for the ride as he did with many dignitaries. Storybook Land's tiny villages were inspired by the architecture of *Pinocchio*, *Cinderella*, and *Alice in Wonderland*. The homes feature real thatched roofs, copper gutters, and tiny stained-glass windows fashioned by Imagineer Harriet Burns. "We ordered all these brooms and cut them up," she recalled about crafting the roofs. "Birds came down to get the thatch off the roofs to make their nests! We'd have to rethatch every now and then."**

RIGHT **An earlier concept for a walk-through Alice attraction was shelved before Disneyland opened, but new ride systems allowed Walt and his Imagineers to revisit earlier ideas when creating new attractions. The inventive three-wheeled caterpillar vehicles of Alice in Wonderland were able to move up and down inclines to carry guests down the rabbit hole and into Wonderland. *Art, Sam McKim***

BELOW **Elizabeth Taylor—accompanied by singer and fourth husband, Eddie Fisher, and their sons in 1959—was a frequent visitor to Disneyland. When it opened in 1958, the exterior design of the Alice in Wonderland attraction differed from most of the other Fantasyland dark rides in that it spanned two levels and featured dimensional set pieces representing the world of the film. Guests would pass giant stylized leaves and blades of grass evocative of Disney artist Mary Blair's concept paintings for the 1951 animated feature.**

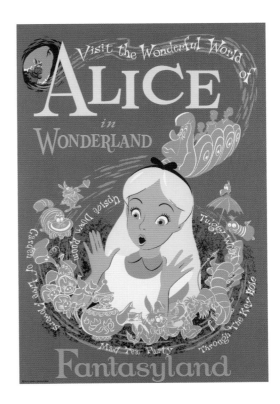

"He usually stands in line like any other tourist and never seems to tire of taking the rides and stopping to talk to children about their likes and dislikes."

—*The Saturday Evening Post*, 1958

ABOVE Hench described how hard it was to capture the "positive qualities" of animated characters in walk-around costumes: "We had to find the right degree of exaggeration to make the walk-around heads large enough to establish the characters identity while relating well to their body size." But the costumes only come to life once donned. "Their static facial expression is overcome by the skill of the cast members...who like dancers or mimes use not only their hands but their whole bodies....Their skill continually astonishes me." *Photo, David Attie*

RIGHT AND BELOW Concept renderings by Bruce Bushman in 1954 envision the cartoony feel of the Casey Jr. Circus Train attraction. As the first art director for the Mickey Mouse Club TV series, Bushman designed much of the show, including the logo that would subsequently adorn the countless Mickey Mouse ear hats sold in Disneyland. *Art, Bruce Bushman*

FOLLOWING A Casey Jr. Circus Train car finds its intended use.

ABOVE **Richard Nixon was born about 10 miles from the future site of Disneyland. Fess Parker greeted the Vice President and his family at City Hall when they arrived about three weeks after opening day in 1955.**

OPPOSITE **Snow White's Adventures was largely designed by Ken Anderson, who came to The Walt Disney Studios in 1934 and contributed to the _Snow White and the Seven Dwarfs_ film. Anderson and fellow animation veteran Claude Coats designed many of the attraction murals in Fantasyland.** *Photo, Loomis Dean*

ABOVE **Mr. Toad's Wild Ride opened with 12 two-seater ride vehicles: Toad, MacBadger, Mole, and Ratty, and two each of Toady, Cyril, Winky and Weasel. They operated at the park until 1997 when they were replaced with four-seaters.** *Photo, Loomis Dean*

OPPOSITE **All it takes is a Peter Pan hat (or Mickey Mouse ears) to transform these guests into children soaring around London on Peter Pan's Flight.** *Photo, Sid Avery*

FOLLOWING **Featured in the 1953** *Peter Pan* **film, Skull Rock debuted in Disneyland in 1960, joining the Chicken of the Sea Pirate Ship, an opening-year restaurant modeled after Captain Hook's galleon.**

"A surprising thing about Disney's paradise for kids is that on some days it is hard to find any bona fide children. Adults — that is, kids eighteen and over — outnumber children almost four to one."

—*The Saturday Evening Post*, 1958

Peter Pan Fly Through.   Castle Courtyard.

*"These classic stories of everyone's youth
have become realities for youngsters
of all ages to participate in."*

—Walt Disney

OPPOSITE When Fantasyland first opened, medieval-inspired tents inspired many of its structures, including the entrance for Peter Pan's Flight. *Art, Herb Ryman*

RIGHT "A great poster sells its story from a distance," said Tony Baxter, "and needs to be glimpsed just briefly to work its magic." The graphic pop of striped sails against the indigo night sky promises an adventure not to missed. *Art, Bjorn Aronson*

BELOW A cutaway attraction layout from 1955 illustrates the final ride path and shows scenes for Peter Pan's Flight as it appeared on opening day. *Art, Bill Martin*

FOLLOWING Unlike the painted flats of other Fantasyland dark rides, the fluorescent set pieces of Peter Pan's Flight had to be dimensional, as riders flying overhead would view them from many angles. *Photo, Thomas Nebbia*

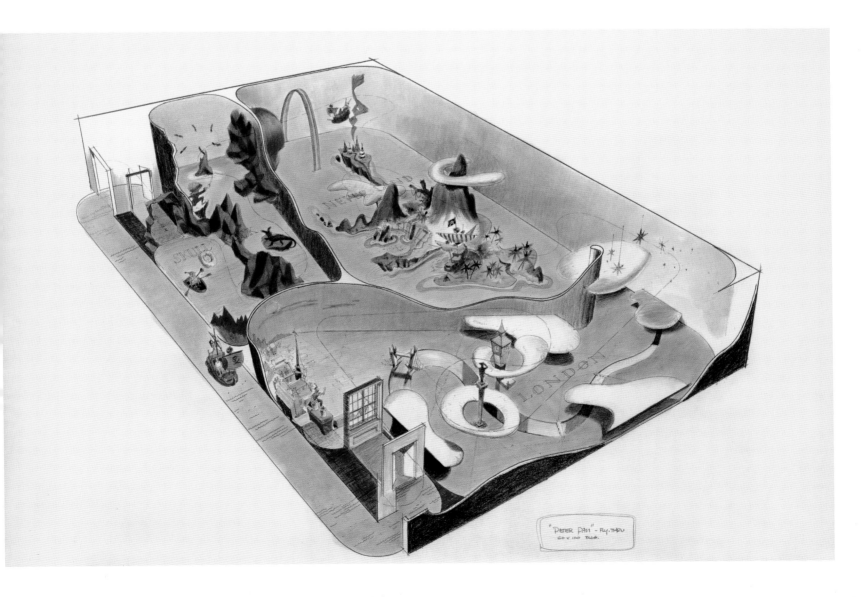

Tomorrowland

Here youth may savor the challenge and promise of the future

Towering above parabolic arches, mosaic tile, and folded plate roofs, the sleek 72-foot (nearly 22 m) white-and-red Moonliner rocket stood poised for blastoff, ready to whisk guests into a world full of advanced science, and modern art. Next stop, Tomorrowland!

The actual rockets that would first carry humans to the moon were built in Downey, California, less than 20 miles (about 32 km) up the Santa Ana Freeway from Tomorrowland. Arriving 14 years before the real thing, Disneyland's Rocket to the Moon attraction made its debut on July 22, 1955. Guests looked down to see Disneyland recede beneath their feet, and up to see the moon growing closer.

Walt's dream of space travel for tourists still seems futuristic by today's standards. Branding it with the logo of a luxury airline, TWA, only added to the authenticity. The spaceship "had to suggest speed and power,"[1] remarked park designer John Hench, and be realistic. Walt hired astrophysicists Willy Ley, Heinz Haber, and Wernher von Braun to consult on the science, from the feel of the phenomenal acceleration to the roar of the engines, and the view of the Earth in the screen below before traveling past a space station at 172,000 miles (almost 277,000 km) per hour. The trio was able to explain complicated systems in layman's terms. "Walt listened wide-eyed," Ward Kimball recounted of a meeting with von Braun, "his mouth open in pure rapture at what he was hearing."[2] The scientists' expertise in spacecraft, space suits, the moon, and

Mars had been popularized in a 1952 *Collier's* magazine series and the book *Across the Space Frontier* before Walt invited them on the Tomorrowland-themed episodes of the *Disneyland* TV show.

Walt called Tomorrowland a "living blueprint of our future" and hired art director Gabriel Scognamillo to realize the details. Scognamillo had recently been nominated for an Academy Award for 1953's *The Story of Three Loves*, but more importantly had created robots and ray guns for the science-fiction film *Tobor the Great* (1954), about a giant robot space pilot controlled by an 11-year-old boy inside a laboratory furnished with Sputnik lamps and Eames chairs. At the entrance to Tomorrowland stood the Clock of the World, an enormous, hourglass-shaped sculpture with a stylized sun and moon revolving around a map of the world.

Kids visiting Tomorrowland in the park's first year could not only take a Rocket to the Moon, they could pilot their own rocket ship on the high-tech Astro-Jets, each vehicle named for the brightest stars in the sky, including: Altair, Procyon, Antares, and Capella. Spaceman K-7 might fly in at any time to greet wandering guests. And from Space Station X-1, visitors could glimpse a view of what the United States might look like from an aerial rotating platform 500 miles (nearly 805 km) above the Earth, a full two years before the Soviet Union launched the world's first satellite, *Sputnik*, into space.

When science and art collide

While space exploration may represent the dreams and hopes of mankind, Tomorrowland reflected the technological revolution happening every day in mid-century America. In 1954, transistors and microwave ovens were introduced, as was the polio vaccine. The United States had also tested the first hydrogen bomb. "Ever since the invention of the bow and arrow," Walt told his television audience, "mankind has been both worried and fascinated by the march of science."[3]

Such advancements were celebrated in Tomorrowland's exhibition halls, sponsored by corporations invested in technology. The Kaiser Hall of Aluminum Fame featured a 40-foot (about 13-m) telescope that guests could walk into and a giant sphere made of aluminum, as well as a life-size model of the goddess Venus draped in aluminum, bathed in colored light, and surrounded by huge, multicolored aluminum stars, representing the fusion of art and industry. A blonde hostess in a metallic minidress might show off Kaiser's latest lightweight aluminum crankcase with the help of KAP, the Kaiser Aluminum Pig.

At Richfield Oil's 1956 exhibition, "The World Beneath Us," visitors learned about the Earth's geological history through a gigantic animated model of its crust, showing powerful underground forces at work. A Technicolor CinemaScope film depicted the explosive origins of the planet, the first appearance of life, the time of dinosaurs, coming of man, and, predictably, the discovery of oil.

And what would washrooms look like in the future? The Crane Company's prediction came in the form of the glamorous 1956 "Bathroom of Tomorrow" exhibit, created by famed industrial designer Henry Dreyfuss, featuring a gold-foil glass-mosaic countertop, 24-karat gold-plated fixtures, and even a swimming pool. An interactive fountain in the forecourt explained the role of valves in seven different industries: petroleum, steam generating, paper pulp, chemical processing, atomic energy, titanium production, and food processing. Guests could turn valves to activate water jets that triggered the movement of a flock of large metal birds and flying saucers; it was art, science, fun, and a little education rolled into one inventive gadget.

At the Monsanto Hall of Chemistry, visitors could "see what chemistry in tomorrow has in store for you," including the Chematron, which featured eight oversized test tubes containing natural substances like salt and water that could be combined to create nearly 500 Monsanto Chemical Company plastics and chemicals. Two years later Monsanto also created an ultramodern dwelling in Tomorrowland made almost entirely from plastic, a showcase for synthetics in the building industry. Up to 10,000 people per day visited the prefabricated Monsanto House of the Future's cantilevered fiberglass modules floating over a garden and waterfalls, near the entrance to Tomorrowland. The home was developed at the Massachusetts Institute of Technology, designed by professors Marvin Goody and

RIGHT Sleek, ultramodern, and predating the launch of the Space Age, this sketch of Tomorrowland offered viewers of Disneyland's October 1954 debut episode a tantalizing glimpse of the future. *Art, Bruce Bushman*

OPPOSITE ABOVE Only at the Disneyland employee cafeteria could one see a Tomorrowland astronaut grabbing a meal with Goofy and Snow White in 1958. Called the Inn Between, it was located behind today's Plaza Inn.

OPPOSITE BELOW A 1959 metal lunch box features two attractions introduced in Tomorrowland that year: the Disneyland-Alweg Monorail and Submarine Voyage.

Richard Hamilton in the Department of Architecture, and highlighted the many uses of man-made materials in the home. Walt offered Monsanto the space to display it when he heard about the prototype.[4]

Air conditioning augmented with the scent of roses or salty sea air was one of the home's unique features, as well as a two-way video phone/intercom, half a century before video chatting became commonplace. Dreyfuss came back to Tomorrowland to design the house's adjustable-height lavatory and a refrigerator and freezer that descended from the kitchen ceiling. The home was also filled with iconic masterpieces of 20th-century modernism: the boy's bedroom featured a Marcel Breuer chair and the living room a multiunit planter designed by George Nelson of the Howard Miller Clock Company. This combination of art, technology, and science to create an idealized space for living likely played into Walt's fascination with such subjects, eventually leading to his desire to design an experimental prototype city of tomorrow in the early 1960s.

The Monsanto House fascinated 20 million guests, including a Russian delegation that built a replica, and a French architect who built his own plastic home. It accomplished its goal as a working prototype providing performance data to the industry. Even though 96 percent of visitors answering a survey said they enjoyed the house, only 0.7 percent cared about the use of plastics. When their 10-year deal with Disneyland was up, Monsanto shifted their sponsorship to another Tomorrowland attraction, Adventure Thru Inner Space. A final testament to the solid design of the House of the Future was reported by *Monsanto* magazine during its 1967 demolition:

Wrecking balls bounced off the tough exterior. And torches, chainsaws, jack-hammers, and clam shovels were similarly ineffective. Finally the crew resorted to choker cables to squeeze the 511,000 pounds [about 232,000 kg] of plastics used in the fiberglass polyester modules into small enough pieces to truck out.[5]

TOMORROW LAND
ENTRANCE

ABOVE At Tomorrowland's entrance stood the Clock of the World, which told time in 24 time zones, its futuristic presence hinting at what was to come in the exhibit halls. Showcased within were innovative technologies created by some of the nation's leading corporations. *Art, Herb Ryman*

Submarines, Monorails, and Autopias!
"Youngsters of all ages" can still drive down the highway of tomorrow on Autopia, one of a handful of opening-day rides operating to this day. Over the years, the attraction has been so popular that it was replicated in three other areas of the park with Midget, Junior, and Fantasyland Autopias. The first Autopia cars were proposed by a German company that sent over a sample it hoped Disney would purchase, but "it left a cloud of smoke behind from the noisy two-cycle

oil-burning engine,"[6] recalled Imagineer Bob Gurr. After designing prototype cars for Ford and writing the 1952 book *How to Draw Cars of Tomorrow*, Gurr was hired by Disney at age 23 to realize a new Autopia car. His team hand-built 37 completely custom vehicles intended for young drivers, including two police cars.

For the rest of Tomorrowland, keeping up with the future was an exciting, ever-evolving process. "During the past few months our artists, designers, engineers,

DESIGNED BY WED ENTERPRISES INC.

DISNEYLAND INC.

and construction people have been hard at work completing Disneyland's biggest expansion program since the Park first opened,"[7] Walt said when describing the 1959 building spree, during which the Disneyland-Alweg Monorail System and Submarine Voyage were introduced. The eight subs were dedicated on June 14 of that year and comprised the world's eighth largest fleet.[8] Hench recalled the view from the submarine lagoon in the '60s:

[It] was dedicated to action, an orchestration of movement, including the aerial Skyway, the surface-level Autopia, the elevated Monorail, and PeopleMover, and the underwater and surface Submarine Voyage. These were all woven into a pattern looping through, around, over, and under each other. The vehicles were streamlined forms with modernistic lines that implied movement. The entire area was staged kinetically to suggest the energy of modern urban life.[9]

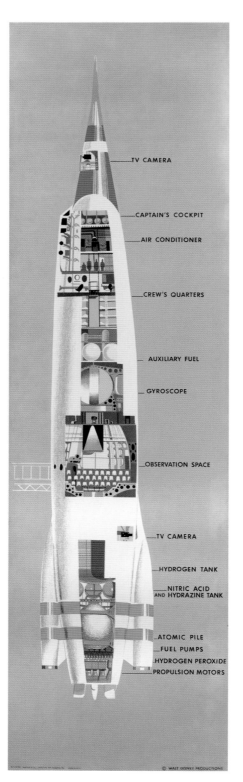

TV CAMERA

CAPTAIN'S COCKPIT

AIR CONDITIONER

CREW'S QUARTERS

AUXILIARY FUEL

GYROSCOPE

OBSERVATION SPACE

TV CAMERA

HYDROGEN TANK

NITRIC ACID AND HYDRAZINE TANK

ATOMIC PILE
FUEL PUMPS
HYDROGEN PEROXIDE
PROPULSION MOTORS

© WALT DISNEY PRODUCTIONS

In a life-imitates-art and art-imitates-life spiral, the 1959 Submarine Voyage opened a year after the United States Navy's nuclear-powered *Nautilus* became the first submarine to travel under the polar ice cap. Park guests could recreate the historic polar voyage on authentic 52-foot (about 16 m) submarines, built with technical assistance from General Dynamics Corporation, suppliers of nuclear submarines to the navy. Traveling through the largest body of filtered water in the world, guests discovered rare specimens of the deep: giant squids, sharks, mermaids, and even a goofy sea serpent. Ruins of ancient civilizations and a sunken treasure were scattered across the ocean floor.

Another transport-themed attraction that, like Autopia, continues to inspire guests to this day is the Monorail, which replaced Tomorrowland's original streamline locomotive, the Viewliner. The sleek trains for the Monorail were based on a prototype by the German Alweg Company and designed with assistance from Lockheed designer Dick Scherer. Gurr added his touch to the body design, inspired by the rocket ships in *Buck Rogers* comics he enjoyed as a kid. As with many Tomorrowland attractions, the Monorail was the first of its kind in the Western Hemisphere and was intended as a realistic preview of transportation in tomorrow's cities. To get to the elevated station, guests rode the Speedramp, a moving sidewalk. Gurr shared his experience leading up to its opening:

> The Monorail did not make an actual trouble-free lap around the track until the night before Walt was to introduce his new monorail system to the world on live TV. The wardrobe department made me a monorail driver's uniform during the night shift. Walt and Art Linkletter showed up with an entourage including Richard Nixon and his family. Walt could get very twinkly eyed and excited when he was showing off something new, and he told everyone about his dream for modern transportation in America. The Secret Service agents were left on the platform (when we departed). Walt and I had kidnapped the Vice President of the United States![10]

A 2.5-mile (approximately 4 km) expansion of the Monorail in 1961 connected guests directly to the Disneyland Hotel outside of the park and was a preview of Walt's idea for a civic mass transit system. He was finally building the future in real life. Now, guests could be transported from their rooms straight into the heart of Tomorrowland.

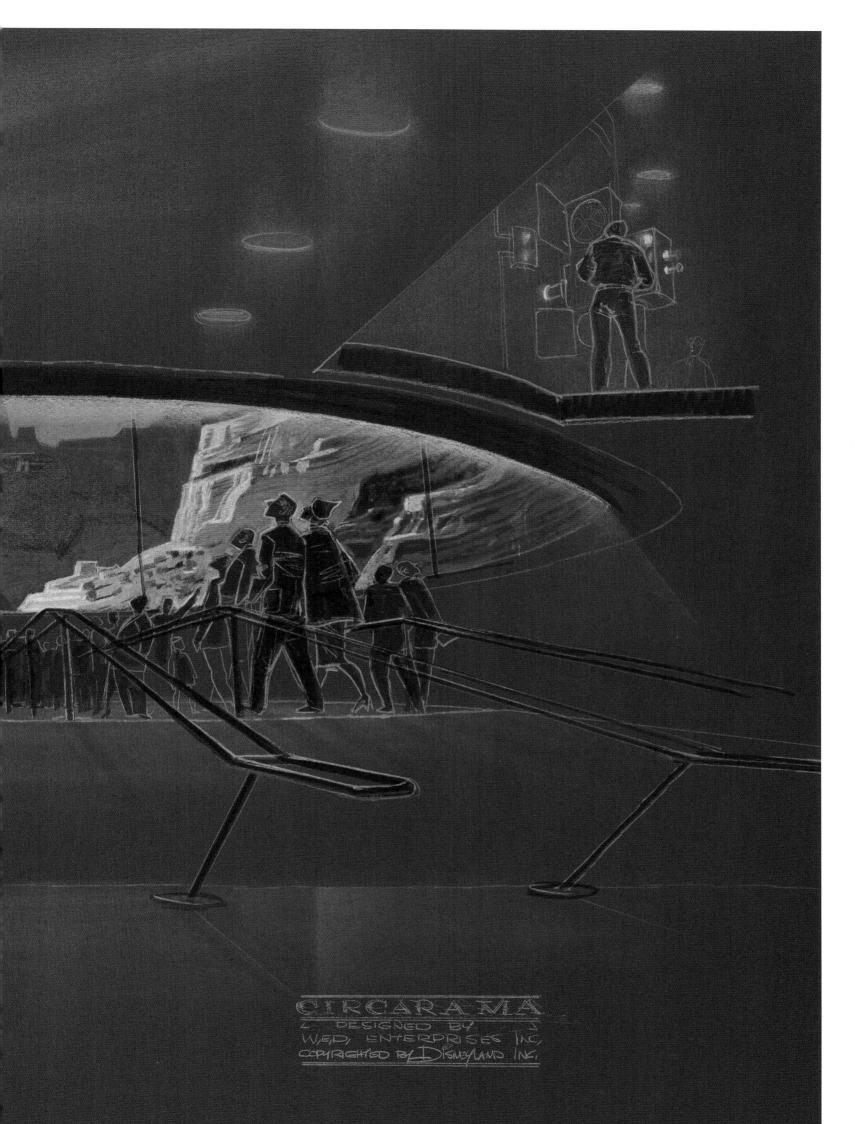

CIRCARAMA
DESIGNED BY
W.E.D. ENTERPRISES INC.
COPYRIGHTED BY DISNEYLAND INC.

PREVIOUS **Multiple film projectors and screens enabled the innovative and seamless 360-degree viewing experience of Circarama, U.S.A., which played the film** *A Tour of the West* **on opening day in 1955.** *Art, John Hench*

ABOVE **The Chematron, the centerpiece of Monsanto's Hall of Chemistry, displayed stylized sculptures of the eight basic materials from which the Monsanto Chemical Company could produce nearly 500 plastics and chemicals.**

OPPOSITE **Like much of the mid-century architecture of Tomorrowland, the folded-plate exterior of the Hall of Chemistry was largely influenced by Italian art director Gabriel Scognamillo, who oversaw the look of the land.**

ABOVE **Fueled by postwar optimism in material science, the Kaiser Hall of Aluminum Fame had numerous wondrous sculptures made of aluminum, including a giant sphere.**

OPPOSITE **Celebrity couple Eddie Fisher and Debbie Reynolds offered Spaceman K-7 a refreshing drink on Disneyland's opening day. By the time of Fisher's next visit in 1958, he had married Elizabeth Taylor.**

ABOVE An early concept rendering for the Rocket to the Moon attraction shows how quickly the modern design aesthetic shifted from the biomorphic lines of early 1950s late moderne to the more hard-edged angular designs realized in Tomorrowland. In the distance looms the *Moonliner*. *Art, Herb Ryman*

OPPOSITE Guests eager to cruise the miniature motorways of Autopia gathered at an entrance of sheet-metal awnings and bent-pipe arches, a design that was simultaneously futuristic and utilitarian. *Art, Herb Ryman*

RICHFIELD AUTOPIA ENTRANCE
DESIGNED BY W.E.D. ENTERPRISES INC.
DISNEYLAND INC.

Copyright
DISNEYLAND INC.

*"Tomorrowland at Disneyland
left a door to the future ajar,
so the public could peer through
before returning to today."*
— **Alan Hess**

OPPOSITE Walk-around character Spaceman K-7 offered Tomorrowland guests a chance to interact with an astronaut. Due to his popularity, Spacegirl later joined him, and the couple roamed the land together greeting visitors. *Photo, David Attie*

RIGHT Walt was a little surprised by the loose and sketchy look of Rolly Crump's Flying Saucer art but encouraged the unusual design. "Walt appreciated creativity," Crump recalled. "For example, he loved Mary Blair's untraditional style." *Art, Rolly Crump*

BELOW Providing guests the opportunity to career around in their own spacecraft, the Flying Saucers were added to Tomorrowland in 1961. They utilized a ride system based on technology similar to that of an air-hockey table, enabling the saucers to float on a thin cushion of air. *Photo, Lawrence Schiller*

LEFT Autopia designer Bob Gurr's book *How to Draw Cars of Tomorrow* was published while he was still a student at Art Center College of Design. *Art, Bob Gurr*

BELOW "If it moves on wheels at Disneyland, I probably designed it," said Bob Gurr, who at 23 was hired to produce the vehicles needed for Autopia, thus beginning his long tenure designing vehicles for the park. *Photo, Lester Nehamkin*

OPPOSITE ABOVE Frank Sinatra and his son, Frank Jr., took a spin on Autopia on Disneyland's opening day. *Photo, Bernie Abramson*

OPPOSITE BELOW The only opening day Tomorrowland attraction still in operation, Autopia has always been a favorite for millions of young drivers. *Art, Bjorn Aronson*

"The bodies bear a...resemblance
to the best lines of Mercedes,
Maserati, Ghia, and others all
rolled into one."

—*Rod and Custom*, 1955

ABOVE Autopia's 37 vehicles had a top speed of 11 miles per hour (about 18 km) and featured two accelerator pedals of varying lengths to ensure that even shorter legs could step on the gas. *Photo, Loomis Dean*

RIGHT The original 1955 Autopia roadway was about one mile long (1.6 km) and two cars wide, allowing drivers to pass each other. Riders navigating this small-scale highway of tomorrow would drive past two large billboards advertising Richfield Oil, then the official gasoline of Disneyland. *Photo, Loomis Dean*

> *"It's not so much a question of 'What happened to the house of the future?' as 'What happened to the future?'"*
>
> —**Aaron Betsky**

ABOVE **When it opened in 1957, the Monsanto House of the Future measured 1,300 square feet (nearly 121 m²), consisted of 20 separate pieces of molded fiberglass, and sat on a 16-square-foot (about 1.5 m²) block of concrete, with utilities running through a central core. More than 20 million guests visited the forward-thinking experiment before its removal in 1967.**

RIGHT Landscaping was important in the design of the attraction. It needed to create a compositional balance between both organic and space-age forms and textures. *Art, John Hench*

BELOW Featuring interiors constructed from molded plastic and filled with sleek mid-century modern fixtures and furniture—designed by the likes of Charles and Ray Eames, Marcel Breuer, and George Nelson—the Monsanto House of the Future was the Case Study House movement meets Disneyland. *Photo, Ralph Crane*

ABOVE Named for its location near the Tomorrowland lagoon and short-lived Phantom Boats attraction, The Yacht Club (later changed to Yacht Bar) was one of the original Tomorrowland eateries, where guests sat in modern, coral-colored fiberglass chairs with built-in tabletops. *Photo, Ralph Crane*

OPPOSITE Corporate partnerships shaped many of the early Tomorrowland attractions and helped make the land itself possible. An exhibit by Bell Telephone System promoted the company's many advances made in telephone technology.

"Tomorrow can be a wonderful age. Our scientists today are opening the doors of the space age to achievements that will benefit our children and generations to come."

—Walt Disney

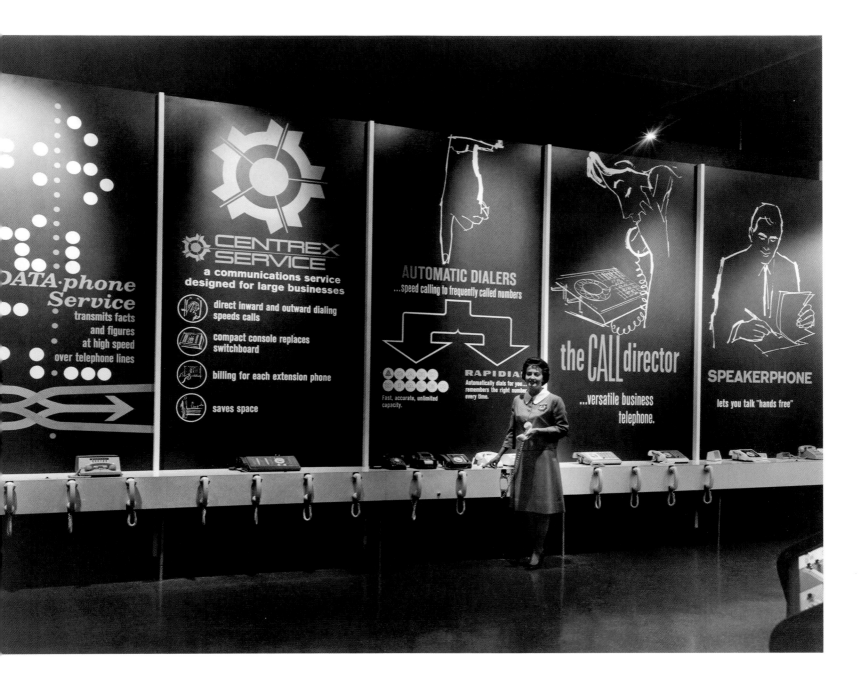

> *"The entire area was staged kinetically to suggest the energy of modern urban life."*
> —John Hench

OPPOSITE **Another early dining option, the Space Bar featured counter service and an array of ultramodern vending machines that dispensed everything from ice cream to hot coffee. Diners sat at tables over-looking the freeways of tomorrow.**

ABOVE **Accomplished art director Gabriel Scognamillo was recruited for Tomorrowland due to his extensive film work, including the sci-fi film** *Tobor the Great.* **Among his unique contributions to the land was a futuristic canopy of pipe arches and discoid shades.** *Photo, Loomis Dean*

"Walt could get very twinkly eyed and excited when he was showing off something new, and he told everyone about his dream for modern transportation in America."

—**Bob Gurr**

OPPOSITE Vice President Richard Nixon and his family dedicated the Monorail on June 14, 1959, with Art Linkletter serving as conductor. Nixon's daughters, Tricia and Julie, were tasked with cutting the ribbon to officially open the ride, but the scissors they were given didn't work. In the end, Walt had to rip off the ribbon.

RIGHT To promote the new Tomorrowland attractions, hand-silkscreened lamppost shields were displayed throughout the park.

BELOW One of the designers of the Monorail, John Hench, said the modes of transportation at Disneyland not only needed to look good in appearance, but also be "a pleasure to watch in action."
Art, Bob Gurr and John Hench

"*During the past few months our artists, designers, engineers, and construction people have been hard at work completing Disneyland's biggest expansion program since the Park first opened...*"

—Walt Disney

See the giant squid from...

20,000 Leagues
UNDER THE Sea

TOMORROWLAND

© WALT DISNEY PRODUCTIONS

OPPOSITE ABOVE **Named for the latest U.S. nuclear subs they were modeled after, the eight original gray subs of Submarine Voyage included *Seawolf*, *Skate*, and *Skipjack*.**

OPPOSITE BELOW **Mermaids greeted guests exploring the Tomorrowland lagoon in 1967. For a few summers, they swam alongside the submarines, enticing guests to board the aquatic attraction. *Photo, Ralph Crane***

ABOVE **Since the *20,000 Leagues Under the Sea* film was popular among audiences, Walt decided to incorporate it into Tomorrowland. Harper Goff was in charge of designing the Nautilus submarine exhibit, an obvious choice as he had just designed the original for the 1954 film. *Art, Bjorn Aronson***

ABOVE The "E" Ticket, which debuted at 50 cents, became synonymous with the best attractions, including the Submarine Voyage, Matterhorn Bobsleds, and Disneyland-Alweg Monorail. *Photo, Lawrence Schiller*

OPPOSITE The Submarine Voyage subs were built with technical assistance from General Dynamics Corporation, suppliers of nuclear submarines to the U.S. Navy. When the ride was dedicated in June 1959, they comprised the world's eighth-largest fleet. *Photo, Ralph Crane*

FOLLOWING Walt had dreams for the Monorail system beyond the park. He believed it could ease traffic in Los Angeles, but Alweg's offer to create a 43-mile system for the city was refused. *Photo, Thomas Nebbia*

The Vision Continues

1964-Today

Walt Dreams
Even Bigger

*With the hope that it will be
a source of joy and inspiration
to all the world*

The 1960s started off as the most productive period in Walt's life. Walt Disney Productions was booming, turning out classic films like 1961's *One Hundred and One Dalmatians, The Absent-Minded Professor*, and *The Parent Trap. Mary Poppins* (1964) won five Academy Awards. WED Enterprises' machine shop headed by Roger Broggie was working double shifts every day; with profits from *Mary Poppins*, Disney started MAPO (its own manufacturing and production division) and purchased an interest in Arrow Development (the park's only ride-system supplier). Arrow was in high demand, even providing habitation modules and life-support systems for the animals in NASA's early rocket tests. Walt was inundated with requests for Disneyland-style transportation systems for cities and shopping malls — including one in 1965 for the La Brea Tar Pits in Los Angeles — which would eventually lead to the formation of a new company called Community Transportation Systems (CTS). Walt developed such an interest in civic life that the author Ray Bradbury, Walt's friend, suggested he run for mayor. "Why should I run for mayor," he replied, "when I am already king of Disneyland?"[1] Work on New Orleans Square, an entirely new land at Disneyland, began in 1962, and, through WED, Walt created four extraordinary attractions for the 1964–65 World's Fair in New York.

"We just can't have too much of the Disney touch at the fair"

Those were the words of legendary New York City urban planner Robert Moses, who served as president of the metropolis's World's Fair. Walt wanted to push artistic and technological innovation to new heights for his New York debut. He built the four attractions — Great Moments with Mr. Lincoln, "it's a small world," the Carousel of Progress, and Magic Skyway — in California and intended to return them after the fair closed to be housed in more permanent structures. Although Magic Skyway didn't come to Disneyland intact, a major portion became Primeval World Diorama, which can still be seen along the Disneyland Railroad.[2] Disney's influence was so integral to the fair that Harper Goff[3] even provided early designs for the globe that became the event's symbol: the Unisphere.[4]

The magnificent *Audio-Animatronics* figure of Abraham Lincoln in the State of Illinois pavilion was particularly remarkable because it was so lifelike. The curtain opened with Lincoln in a seated position, he then rose to engage the audience in a conversation about liberty. As Walt mentions in a 1964 episode of *Walt Disney's Wonderful World of Color*, he was excited to showcase new technology his company developed:

> *Disneyland gave us a new art and a new type of artist — one that works with a slide rule and blowtorch instead of pencil and brush. Just as we had to learn to make our animated cartoons talk, we had to find a way to make [attraction figures] talk, too. We created a new type of animation.*[5]

Lincoln's movements were choreographed by Marc Davis and other animation veterans,

Great Moments with Mr. Lincoln was the first of the World's Fair creations to arrive back at Disneyland. The Main Street Opera House became its new home in time for Disneyland's 10th anniversary Tencennial celebration in 1965.

Bradbury shared his feelings about seeing Lincoln while visiting the "Disney robot factory":

> *In such an age it would be foolhardy to ignore the one man who is building human qualities into robots — robots whose influence will be ricocheting off social and political institutions ten thousand afternoons from today. ... Disney has set the history of humanized robots on its way toward wider, more fantastic excursions into the needs of civilization. Send your mind on to the year 2065. ... with a group of children entering an audio animatronic museum ... Emerging from the robot museums of tomorrow, your future student will say: "I know, I believe in the history of the Egyptians, for this day I helped lay the cornerstone of the Great Pyramid" ... The new appreciation of history begins with the responsibility in the hands of a man I trust, Walt Disney ... [and] in the robots that Disney, and others long after him, invent and send forth upon the land.[7]*

Of all the innovations introduced at the New York World's Fair, increased ride capacity was perhaps most important to future operations at Disneyland. More than 50 million people visited the fair in its two seasons — at a time when Disneyland saw an average of six million visitors a year.[8] Arrow Development created the tracked boats for "it's a small world" and the rotating theater for Carousel of Progress, which could each handle twice as many guests as any other attraction in the park.

For the look of "it's a small world," Walt enlisted the help of painter and designer Mary Blair, who had inspired the art direction of *Cinderella* (1950), *Alice in Wonderland* (1951), and *Peter Pan* (1953). Blair brought her bold color choices to the interior of the attraction, selecting different schemes for each nation, and setting the overall design aesthetic. Rolly Crump was charged with translating Blair's aesthetic into a three-dimensional space and designed the 120-foot-tall (about 37 m) kinetic Tower of the Four Winds sculpture in front of the New York version of the show, which Walt described as representing "the boundless energy of youth."

ABOVE **According to Imagineer Marty Sklar, the day the New York World's Fair opened was almost the exact day that Disney purchased the first piece of land in central Florida. At the fair, Walt tried out four new attractions: "it's a small world," Great Moments with Mr. Lincoln, the Carousel of Progress, and Magic Skyway. They allowed his Imagineers to test new technologies and prepare an East Coast audience for what would become Walt Disney World.**

OPPOSITE **At first, Imagineers considered what the Carousel of Progress theater might look like floating on a series of modernist pilotis. In the end, it lived on the ground floor. *Art, John Hench***

but the finely controlled mechanics relied on cutting-edge machinery. These were the world's first humanoid *Audio-Animatronics* figures, and they were all handmade: "[They] were built first, then designed," remembered Imagineer Bob Gurr. "We would make manufacturing drawings only after the parts were built and shown to work." The Lincoln figure had 13 structural units, each moving in a different direction. "All of this stuff had to fit inside this tall, skinny Lincoln," said Gurr. "Oh gosh, why didn't Walt want Grover Cleveland?!"[6] To create the figure's movement, actor Royal Dano was filmed from multiple angles. Gurr ran the film frame by frame, made paper tracings on the screen, and took the tracings to drafters who made production drawings, which were finally sent to the shop. Sculptor Blaine Gibson worked from an original life mask cast in 1860 from the face of the 16th president. More than two million people saw the exhibit at the fair, and some were moved to tears by the power of the presentation.

"Well, it's beautiful," Walt told the Sherman Brothers on a walk-through prior to its opening at the World's Fair. "But we've got a problem."[9] The original soundtrack consisted of dozens of national anthems played over one another.

"On paper it sounds good," remembers Richard M. Sherman. "But it was the biggest mess…He starts giving us a lecture about this ride and he used the words 'the small children of the world are the hope of the future, but you have to say it simple like a folk song.' He said it should be a roundelay."[10] The brothers, who had studied music at Bard College, came up with a solution for Walt:

How about a counterpoint? That's two melodies that interlock on the same cantus firmus, on the same chord construction. They work together or separately. Sometimes you hear the children singing "it's a small world" and sometimes you hear "There is just one moon" and sometimes you hear them both together and it's very natural. We would change from a German band to Japanese style. It's the same song in the same tempo but very different. You get the feeling of traveling around the world.…It's like painting with sound.[11]

"Mr. Disney…remind[s] us in song of the brotherhood of men all over the world," actress Carol Channing told the press at the opening. "All of the dolls have the same face, though their color is different."[12] She was clearly moved, and the playful homage to the children of the world continues to enchant audiences as a sparkling ode to peace.

When the ride was moved back to Disneyland without its massive signature sculpture, Walt called Crump again: "The façade is my interpretation of Mary Blair in my style."[13] Blair and Crump also worked alongside Claude Coats, who designed the layout; Marc Davis, who worked on animation; and Marc's wife, Alice, who created the costumes. Bank of America took over sponsorship from Pepsi-Cola and UNICEF, and a new four-story building was raised where more than 500 *Audio-Animatronics* children, toys, and animals from more than 100 regions of the world could sing together in Anaheim.

The Sherman Brothers would compose another earworm for the Carousel of Progress, the main attraction of the General Electric pavilion, which would reopen in Tomorrowland in 1967. In four acts the show tells the story of how electricity changed the way we live. We see the same family as

"We just can't have too much of the Disney touch at the Fair."

— Robert Moses

CAROUSEL THEATRE · TOMORROWLAND

ABOVE The Carousel of Progress celebrated the technological advances of the 20th century by following an American family through several generations. The final scene illustrates Space Age optimism for a "great big beautiful tomorrow." *Art, Collin Campbell*

OPPOSITE LEFT Like the other World's Fair attractions that "came home" to Disneyland, the Carousel of Progress show was built entirely in California, shipped to New York, and then shipped back to California. *Art, Ken Chapman*

OPPOSITE RIGHT Inspired by the play *Our Town*, in which a singular narrator tells the story, the General Electric attraction was narrated by an *Audio-Animatronics* father named John.

RIGHT Sculptor Blaine Gibson based the "father" figure on a life cast of TV actor Preston Hanson. He and the family dog appear in the same spot in the kitchen of 1900, 1920, 1940, and "today."

their home evolves (with GE appliances) throughout the 20th century: the gaslit world of 1900; the 1920s, when radio arrived in the home; 1940s, the birth of television; and the present day, showing the latest household innovations. What was particularly unique about the design of the space was that instead of the stage moving around the audience, the audience revolved around a fixed stage. Richard M. Sherman wrote the lyrics to the pavilion's theme song, "There's a Great Big Beautiful Tomorrow," and his brother, Robert, wrote the music, arranging it in the style of the four time periods. Richard recalled the first time Walt showed them the model for the attraction:

> *Walt was the most enthusiastic salesman you ever met in your life. He could sell ice in the winter, and he was getting us so steamed up. He said, 'I want you to write me a song that could transport you to these different eras,' and I said to Bob, 'Walt has a dream and that's the start,' and Bob said, 'Man that sounds like a song lyric!' He always thought tomorrow would be marvelous.*[14]

The Magic Skyway, designed by Vic Greene and John Hench, was the highest-capacity ride at the fair thanks to a new ride system. Here, an endlessly moving loop of 160 brand-new Ford convertibles traveled from the dawn of time to the city of tomorrow along a fixed track. Along the way, passengers viewed the primeval world, populated with

prehistoric beasts, some of which were later installed adjacent to the Grand Canyon Diorama on the Santa Fe and Disneyland Railroad, and met the caveman who created the wheel. Yale Gracey, who had been a layout artist at the studio, created part of the preshow: an infinity room filled with Ford Model Ts using a special-effects technique called a Pepper's Ghost (a method he later used for the endlessly dancing celebrants at the Haunted Mansion). The Magic Skyway was the only Disney-designed World's Fair exhibit that was left behind at the fair; however, bits of it did make it back to Disneyland, including the new mode of transport, some of the special-effects ideas, and those *Audio-Animatronics* dinosaurs.

Transforming life's fantasies into living fantastically

The year 1965 was an especially busy one for Walt. He poured himself into the development of a year-round alpine ski and recreation resort — which would never be built — at Mineral King, a spectacular mountain area in the Sierra Nevada mountains about 200 miles (about 322 km) from Los Angeles. There was a big celebration for the 10th anniversary of the park that became a television special. And Walt publicly announced his most utopian dream yet: the Experimental Prototype Community of Tomorrow (EPCOT), which he described as "always in the state of becoming."[15]

The idea began to crystalize for Walt in 1959, when Los Angeles architect Victor Gruen, known as the "father of the shopping mall," proposed a "city of the future" concept for an alternate 1964 World's Fair near Washington, D. C. Gruen's plan called for 4,500 acres (about 1821 ha) of open land, parking, and transportation to encircle a 600-acre (nearly 243 ha), pedestrian-only core of exhibition buildings, with support systems hidden below. It was designed to outlive the fair and become a working city in Largo, Maryland. Walt's plans for EPCOT, including a radial plan and hidden transportation systems with a central business core surrounded by rings of green belts and high- and low-density housing, were clearly influenced by Gruen's vision. Walt wondered why some of the technology he saw when visiting corporate research laboratories never made it to the public and thought communities like EPCOT could work together with companies for real-world testing of new ideas.

That same year, 1959, a billionaire investor had proposed a second Disneyland

ABOVE **Sculptor Blaine Gibson used a life mask of Abraham Lincoln, cast in 1860 by Leonard Volk, as reference to authentically capture the 16th president's face. The performance of the *Audio-Animatronics* President Lincoln so moved guests at the World's Fair that *The New York Times* reported, "many visitors insist the Disney figure is human."**

OPPOSITE **Imagineers recorded the intricate animation on a series of magnetic tapes synched to actor Royal Dano's vocal performance. During the development of the Lincoln figure, Walt said, "There must be some way…some undeveloped means of communication…perhaps some new art form that can combine the best of traditional media…to present the courage and strength of Abraham Lincoln." Lincoln's armature alone featured 13 fully contained moving structural units.** *Photo, Thomas Nebbia*

"Disney has set the history of humanized robots on its way toward wider, more fantastic excursions into the needs of civilization."

—Ray Bradbury

RIGHT **Martin Luther King, Jr. visited the Ford Magic Skyway at the New York World's Fair with his children Yolanda and Martin III in August of 1964.**

BELOW **Magic Skyway featured a perpetual moving chain of 160 Ford convertibles that conveyed guests from the dawn of time to the city of tomorrow. This high-capacity ride system led to the Omnimover ride technology later implemented in Adventure Thru Inner Space and Haunted Mansion attractions at Disneyland. It was the only Disney-designed World's Fair attraction of the four that wasn't moved to Disneyland. However, various pre-historic *Audio-Animatronics* from the pavilion did find a new home in the Primeval World Diorama at Disneyland.** *Photo, John G. Zimmerman*

[almost 18 km] in the other."[16] He had so much land he would call his new carefully planned region Disney World.

Disneyland will never be complete

Despite the demands on his time, Walt still managed to spend time at Disneyland, walking the grounds in the early morning hours, making sure everything was up to his standards. As if creating four innovative attractions for the World's Fair wasn't enough, Walt was completely redesigning Tomorrowland and overseeing construction of New Orleans Square, which had begun in 1962 and was finally dedicated on July 24, 1966.

Victor Schiro, the mayor of New Orleans, joined Walt at the grand opening on a beautiful summer day as Dixieland music filled the air courtesy of the Firehouse Five Plus Two, including animator Ward Kimball on the trombone. The politician pinned a medal on Walt, proclaiming him an honorary citizen of the Crescent City and offering him the mayor's chair.

The neighborhood of winding streets and iron-lace balconies was filled with specialty shops like Mlle. Antoinette's Parfumerie and Cristal D'Orleans, where craftsmen made and sold cut glass. The food of the Old South was available at the Creole Cafe, Le Gourmet, and the highly atmospheric Blue Bayou Restaurant, a lavish theme restaurant set on the waterfront built entirely inside the centerpiece of the new land: Pirates of the Caribbean.

The classic journey down the waterfall and through a ransacked, burning town with drunken buccaneers was originally planned as a walk-through wax museum and was not ready to debut until the following March. More than 70 *Audio-Animatronics* figures filled the pirate ships, town, and jail, some more detailed than others. Marc Davis remembered questioning Walt about "the highly developed auctioneer figure," whose subtle movements would likely go unnoticed by guests as it was impossible for them to closely examine the figures from the confines of the moving boats. "Walt said, 'Hey look, Marc, that's great. You know we get so much repeat business here. That means each time we come down we'll see something that we didn't see before.'"[17]

The opening of New Orleans Square would unfortunately be Walt's last dedication at his beloved park. A few months later, on November 2, 1966, Walt went to St. Joseph's Hospital in Burbank because he was experiencing pain in his leg and

in Palm Beach, Florida. Perhaps that was the place to build EPCOT. So again Walt hired "Buzz" Price who had scouted the location for Disneyland. And in 1963 Price determined that central Florida, not Palm Beach, had the best access to tourism. Two years later, Disney purchased more than 27,000 acres (almost 11,000 ha) there. Walt needed so much land because he was planning an airport, transportation system, industrial park, entertainment center (later called the Magic Kingdom), and most importantly his dream city, EPCOT. "It'll be like standing on top of the Matterhorn," Walt told Dick Nunis, who later would become executive vice president of operations for the new park. "And looking seven miles [about 11 km] in one direction and 11 miles

"People don't walk out of the attraction whistling the architecture."

—John Hench

neck, which news reports attributed to an old polo injury. During the examination, a tumor was discovered on his left lung, and Walt would soon return to have it removed along with a portion of his lung. "It took everybody by surprise, including my father," Diane Disney told an interviewer. "He didn't know that he had lung cancer."[18]

Walt spent Thanksgiving with his family but was back at St. Joseph's for his 65th birthday on December 5. He would not leave again. The day before he passed, his brother Roy recalled, "Walt lay on the hospital bed staring at the ceiling. It was squares of perforated acoustical tile, and Walt pictured them as a grid map for Disney World.... Every four tiles represented a square mile, and he said, 'Now there is

where the highway will run. There is the route for the monorail.' He drove himself right up to the end."[19]

Walt Disney died at 9:35 A.M. on December 15, 1966, of "acute circulatory collapse," according to the hospital. The studio closed at noon that day. "When I got home it really hit me," Imagineer Xavier "X" Atencio recalled. "I just sat in my room and I just bawled like a baby."[20]

Tributes poured in from all over the world. Walt's friend Ronald Reagan said, "There just aren't any words to describe my personal grief."[21] "The world is a poorer place now," producer Samuel Goldwyn reflected. "But in a larger sense Walt Disney has not died because he will live for all time through his work."[22]

OPPOSITE **Brothers Robert B. (standing) and Richard M. (at the piano) Sherman composed and arranged the theme songs for two World's Fair attractions that would find permanent homes at Disneyland: the eponymous theme of "it's a small world" and "There's a Great Big Beautiful Tomorrow" from the Carousel of Progress. John Hench said of the importance of music, "People don't walk out of the attraction whistling the architecture."**

BELOW **Artist Mary Blair and Walt study a component of the "it's a small world" scale model for Disneyland.**

ABOVE AND LEFT **When Walt Disney agreed to create "it's a small world" for the New York World's Fair, he remembered the playful drawings of Mexican children by Mary Blair for the 1945 animated film *The Three Caballeros*. Blair had been a color stylist and designer at The Walt Disney Studios during the 1940s and early 1950s, before going on to become a graphic designer and children's book illustrator. Walt invited her back to design the attraction in the same style.** *Art, Mary Blair*

OPPOSITE **Fellow designer Rolly Crump said of Blair's involvement in the project, "It was a powerful package for her. It was about children, the freedom of color, and that Walt had asked her to do it. Like she'd died and gone to heaven."** *Art, Mary Blair*

OPPOSITE **Imagineer Rolly Crump (left) designed the 120-foot-tall (about 37 m) Tower of the Four Winds that served as the exterior icon of "it's a small world" during its run at the World's Fair. Representing "the boundless energy of youth," Walt was fascinated with whirligigs and mobiles Crump had created at the studio. The tower was left behind at the end of the fair and a new façade was designed for Disneyland.**

RIGHT AND BELOW **Mary Blair's color studies for the iconic ride simultaneously radiate a playful sense of childlike wonder while displaying a mastery of the colorful and graphic mid-century modern design aesthetic that reached its peak in the mid-1960s.** *Art, Mary Blair*

ABOVE **Pepsi-Cola had sponsored the original attraction in New York, but Bank of America, under the direction of board chairman Louis Lundberg (pictured), sponsored the rebuild of the attraction in Anaheim.**

LEFT **"The key to the success of 'it's a small world' was that in creating it, we all remained faithful to the mood and feel of Mary's design," said Crump, who was tasked with translating Blair's whimsical illustrations into three-dimensional environments and set pieces.** *Art, Mary Blair*

RIGHT In 1963, costume designer Alice Davis, who was married to Imagineer Marc Davis, was hired by Walt to create 150 costumes for the World Fair's "it's a small world." She only had kind words to share of her experience: "Walt was a marvelous boss because he knew what you could do more so than you did."

BELOW Walt also asked Blair to design a clock tower for the entrance to the attraction at Disneyland. During a plane ride from New York to Los Angeles, she sketched an idea on a small scrap of paper that would ultimately evolve (with input from Crump) into the iconic facade that debuted in 1966. "Usually I begin by making little doodle sketches to plan the overall design and pattern," Blair remembered.

OPPOSITE **Bordering Adventureland and Frontierland is New Orleans Square, whose exterior architecture of tonally reserved hues—chosen to give the land a feeling of romantic patina and baroque character—contrasts with the bright facades of Main Street, U.S.A.** *Art, Herb Ryman*

ABOVE **Artist Dorothea Redmond executed many of the interior and exterior renderings of New Orleans Square, joining Herb Ryman in setting the aesthetic tone of the land. This included the completely indoor Blue Bayou Restaurant, a moody romantic waterfront eatery where it is always twilight.** *Art, Dorothea Redmond*

RIGHT **Since the opening of the park, Walt Disney maintained a small private apartment above the Main Street fire station. Plans for New Orleans Square included a larger personal residence that would overlook the new land. Drawn in 1965, this elegant section elevation showcases the air-conditioned interior patio for the apartment, which was built above the entrance to the Pirates of the Caribbean attraction.** *Art, Dorothea Redmond*

THIS SPREAD A trio of 1965 watercolor concepts of New Orleans Square destinations demonstrates Dorothea Redmond's evocative style. "All the great art directors, like Bill Martin and Harper Goff, wanted Dorothea's design illustrations," Marty Sklar once said. She did not just create illustrations, "but living environments." Walt felt the architecture of New Orleans would be a nice addition along with Rivers of America's banks. When the new land opened in 1966, it transported guests to the city as it looked a century ago. Visitors shopped at the One of a Kind shop for hard-to-find antiques and could even have personalized blends of perfume made at Mlle. Antoinette's Perfumerie. *Art, Dorothea Redmond*

OPPOSITE Walt Disney wrote, "From the lacy iron grillwork of its balconies to the sound of a Dixieland jazz band . . . New Orleans Square recalls her namesake, the fabled 'Queen of the Delta,' as it was a century ago . . ."

ABOVE The unique atmosphere of the Blue Bayou Restaurant continues to charm guests as it did when it first opened in 1967, with fine dining by candlelight, as fireflies blink about in the perpetual night sky, and the calming sounds of the bayou.

RIGHT The designers of New Orleans Square aimed to create an authentic old-world feeling to the new land, and different intimate dining options were integral to that. *Art, Marc Davis*

NEW ORLEANS SQUARE

ABOVE Situated near the exit of the Pirates of the Caribbean attraction, the Pirates Arcade Museum challenged guests to test their skill on a series of custom-themed wooden-cabinet arcade games, designed to mix fact and fun. *Art, Dorothea Redmond*

OPPOSITE A block of New Orleans Square buildings displays the muted color palette used to infuse the land with a character of age specific to the Crescent City. *Art, Dorothea Redmond*

RIGHT This concept drawing for Captain Hook's treasure hunt was realized as a shooting gallery arcade game which played the song "A Pirate's Life" from *Peter Pan*. *Art, Sam McKim*

WALT DREAMS EVEN BIGGER

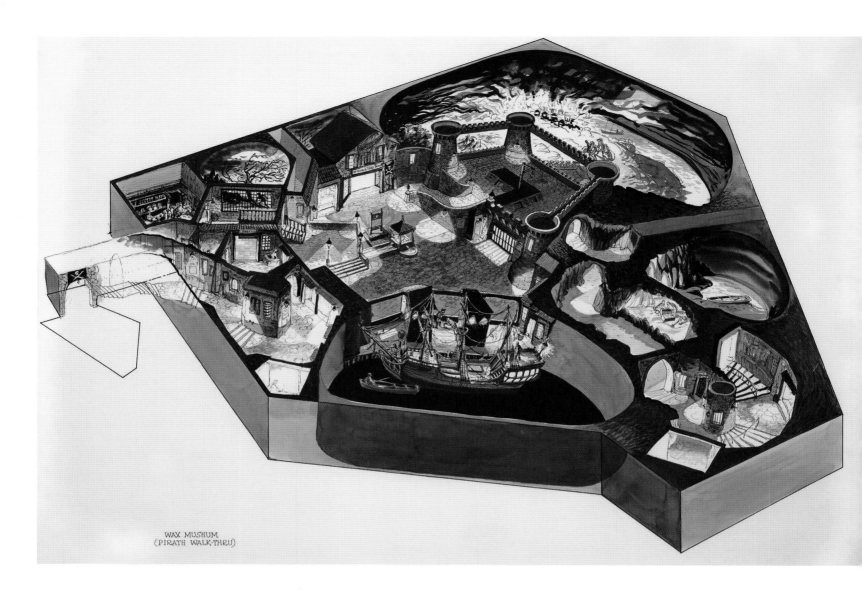

WAX MUSEUM
(PIRATE WALK-THRU)

Captain's Quarters   "Pirates of the Caribbean"

ABOVE Marc Davis, one of Walt Disney's legendary "Nine Old Men" of animation, was recruited to WED Enterprises in 1962. One of his first assignments was to design concepts for a walk-through pirate wax museum that was to be located under New Orleans Square. Many of the elements in his 1963 plan were adapted to fit into the final ride-through Pirates of the Caribbean attraction that opened in 1967. *Art, Marc Davis*

LEFT A concept sketch for the captain's quarters displays Davis's ability for creating memorable scenes that instantly communicate story and tone to guests in passing boats. *Art, Marc Davis*

RIGHT Pirates of the Caribbean uses humor to tackle what might otherwise be grim subject matter. "They were having fun," according to X Atencio, who penned the attraction's script. "They were just a bunch of fun-loving pirates." An ominous Jolly Roger, voiced by Atencio, warns guests they might encounter plunderin' pirates just as their boat splashes into the caverns below. *Art, Marc Davis*

BELOW An early 1962 concept for the planned pirates walk-through attraction featured real pirates Anne Bonny and Mary Read admiring their treasure. Though the pair and all historical figures were cut from the ride-through version, the rest of the remains largely intact in the scene. *Art, Marc Davis*

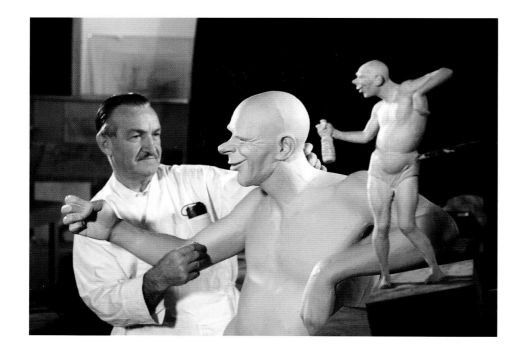

LEFT Using Marc Davis's sketches as reference, small-scale maquettes were crafted to bring the characters of Pirates of the Caribbean into dimensional form. Sculptor George Snowden references a miniature drunken pirate while sculpting the full-scale figure that would inhabit the burning-village scene.

BELOW One of the original members of the WED Model Shop, Harriet Burns helped construct the scale models for Pirates of the Caribbean so that Walt could study every detail from the point of view of guests riding the finished attraction.

OPPOSITE The *Audio-Animatronics* figures for Pirates of the Caribbean were produced by MAPO, a new subsidiary of WED Enterprises named after the 1964 Disney feature *Mary Poppins*, whose profits helped fund the division in 1965.

ROGUES' GALLERY
FAMOUS PIRATES
OF THE SPANISH MAIN

CAPTAIN JOHN EVERY — "LONG BEN"

*"Disneyland gave us a new art
and a new type of artist — one that
works with a slide rule and blowtorch
instead of pencil and brush."*

—Walt Disney

ABOVE "Pirates of the Spanish Main"
was one of the several working titles
used while developing the pirates
attraction as a walk-through wax-
museum concept. *Art, Bruce Bushman*

LEFT Another early Davis sketch of
real British pirate "Captain John
Every" — a hybrid of the pirate's
original name, Henry Every and alias
John Avery — is notable for the cross-
stitch reading "Dead Men Tell No
Tales," a line the iconic talking Jolly
Roger says to the millions of guests
who ride Pirates of the Caribbean.
Art, Marc Davis

RIGHT **Three months before the Pirates of the Caribbean opening, the crew lost their captain when Walt Disney passed away in December of 1966. Although Walt never experienced the finished attraction, it represents the last addition to Disneyland he completely oversaw.**

BELOW **Miles of electrical wiring and hydraulic lines were installed by Imagineers to bring the incredible sights and sounds of Pirates of the Caribbean, still one of the park's most beloved attractions, to life.**

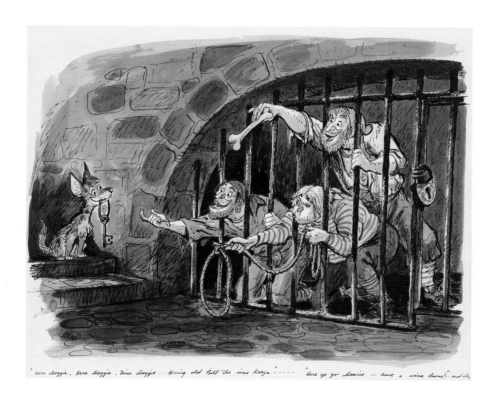

ABOVE When X Atencio approached Walt concerned that he had written too much dialogue for the attraction. Marty Sklar remembered Walt telling Atencio, "Think of it this way. You're at a giant cocktail party and you go through and you pick up this voice over here, and the voice over here, and somebody talking about this over here, but you don't get it all. So you have to go back and you have to ride it again." *Art, Claude Coats*

OPPOSITE AND RIGHT **Marc Davis's humorous concept scenes informed the design and animation of the figures that performed in Claude Coats's rich environments. Their tactful balance of comical vignettes and grim scenarios was later masterfully repeated in their collaboration on the Haunted Mansion.** *Art, Marc Davis*

FOLLOWING **Pirates of the Caribbean set a park-attendance record in the wake of Walt Disney's death, and helped erase doubts about the future of Disneyland without Walt at the helm. According to Alice Davis, "Pirates of the Caribbean literally saved Disneyland."** *Photo, Ralph Crane*

3 CAPTIVES AND GUARD

Disneyland Is Your Land

Life after Walt

"Walt Disney was not just a dreamer whose visions like Disneyland came true," his brother Roy recounted in the 1967 Walt Disney Productions Annual Report. "He was a creative planner…[reaching] five, ten, even twenty years ahead."[1] After more than two decades of dreaming, developing, and realizing the Happiest Place on Earth, Walt Disney had died at the age of 65, leaving an indelible mark on the lives of millions around the world through his film and television work, but especially through the legacy of Disneyland. Following Walt's death, his brother Roy continued as president and chairman of Walt Disney Productions, and oversaw WED Enterprises.

Dick Nunis, director of park operations, remembered being called to Roy's office a short time later. "Well, Dick, whaddya think?" the new president of WED Enterprises asked him. "Can we do it without Walt?" Nunis replied, "Sir, I don't know, but I think we ought to try."[2] The visionary was gone, but his vision continued.

The Disney family still owned about 34 percent[3] of the publicly traded company. Roy expressed his commitment to the park at the company's annual meeting held in February 1967. "We have no intentions to merge or sell out," he assured shareholders. "We'd be foolish to take a step like that… It would be the company's ruination."[4]

True to Roy's word, Disneyland bustled with activity in the months that followed. Pirates of the Caribbean, which was not finished during Walt's last appearance at the park, opened on March 18. The attraction was an immediate hit with such staying power that it eventually inspired the popular live-action movie franchise of the same name. (The phenomena would come full circle when characters from the movie — including Johnny Depp as Captain Jack Sparrow — were added to the original scenes at Disneyland in 2006.)

But July 2, 1967, would mark an even bigger debut: an entirely new Tomorrowland. "When we opened Disneyland, outer space was *Buck Rogers*," Walt had said in 1966 of the decision to reimagine the land. "And since then has come *Sputnik* and then…our great program in outer space. So I had to tear down my Tomorrowland that I built 11 years ago and rebuild it to keep pace."[5] Every attraction except Autopia, Submarine Voyage, the Monorail, and Skyway was demolished or rebuilt.

By the time the new Tomorrowland opened, John Glenn had orbited the Earth, and tests were underway on the *Saturn V* rocket that would propel the Apollo astronauts to the moon. "To design the future, we relied on then current science-fiction illustrations," noted John Hench. "Trips to Bell Labs and NASA, where we could talk with people actively working on projects and products for the future, also stimulated our imaginations."[6]

Officials from the biggest corporations in America were there to celebrate the land's reopening; many had a hand in making it a reality. General Electric's Carousel of

ABOVE **Continuing the tradition set in the original Tomorrowland, the new attractions were created in partnership with many of the nation's leading corporations. Bell Telephone System sponsored** *America the Beautiful,* **a Circle-Vision 360 film that also included an exhibition of the company's video-phone technology.**

OPPOSITE **Adventure Thru Inner Space ended with a word from our sponsor. This display space would showcase clothing made with Monsanto space-age miracle fibers. The company stopped making polyester in 1981.** *Art, T. Hee*

Progress was now back in California after its two-year stay at the 1964–65 New York World's Fair; Monsanto's Adventure Thru Inner Space, which delved into the world of subatomic-particle physics, would have guests riding Atomobiles through a giant microscope as they shrank down to the size of an atom; the Bell Telephone Systems– sponsored *America the Beautiful,* a new film produced in Circle-Vision 360; and a new animatronic tour guide, Tom Morrow, greeted visitors from the new mission-control room in the Flight to the Moon attraction, an up- date of Rocket to the Moon. The sponsorships continued throughout Tomorrowland with Goodyear partnering on the PeopleMover, a transportation system that took 5,000 passengers per hour on an elevated beam through the Bell, Monsanto, and General Electric pavilions. Coca-Cola backed the new Tomorrowland Terrace, which showcased a moving, outdoor sculpture garden made of concrete, which rose to reveal a stage below, and featured dining, dancing, and live en- tertainment. Perhaps the most appropriate

gathering in the history of the land happened on July 20, 1969, when capacity crowds gathered for a live broadcast of the Apollo 11 moon landing at the Tomorrowland Stage.

That same summer, Disneyland's first private club, Club 33, also opened in New Orleans Square. It was a fine-dining destina- tion with a full cocktail menu, another first in the park. Originally Walt envisioned the club as a place to entertain executives and their guests and to provide a secure place for visiting dignitaries, but at times member- ships have been offered to the public. For example, for the club's 45th anniversary in 2012 they became available for an initial cost of $25,000 and annual dues of $10,000.[7] The waiting list for membership was so long that the intimate club was expanded in 2015 to increase capacity.

Everyone was welcomed at the Haunted Mansion, which can be found in even the earliest sketches for Disneyland. The happy haunt went through many iterations before finally opening in the square in 1969. Rolly Crump remembers most of the early ideas

ABOVE **Concept sketches for Monsanto's Adventure Thru Inner Space imagined Atomobile ride vehicles and postshow exhibits heralding new "Miracles from Molecules" from Monsanto.** *Art, George McGinnis*

OPPOSITE **A Trip Through a Drop of Water was an early concept for a Tomorrowland attraction—also referred to as Micro World—that evolved and eventually became Adventure Thru Inner Space.** *Art, John Hench*

FOLLOWING SPREAD **A series of concept sketches from 1966 illustrate dramatic scenes in the attraction when guests pass through Monsanto's Mighty Microscope into the nucleus of an atom. "For although your body will shrink," narrator Paul Frees intoned, "your mind will expand."** *Art, X Atencio and Claude Coats (bottom left)*

for the mansion being "pretty corny" takes on haunted-house clichés, not much more than banging shutters and secret panels. Crump's own Museum of the Weird concept, which included characters like the melting candle man and a beastly chair that could talk to guests, never got past the model stage. Eventually, designer Claude Coats, who wanted a scary haunted house, and colleague Marc Davis, whose designs were more humorous, went to work with illusion expert Yale Gracey and songwriter X Atencio, who wrote the theme song "Grim Grinning Ghosts," to create a slowly winding Doom Buggy ride through a graveyard, attic, and ballroom where happy haunts materialize for a swinging wake. Don't try to hide or a silly spook may sit by your side.

Another world rises

In 1968, Roy O. Disney resigned as president of Walt Disney Productions.[8] Donn Tatum (president), E. Cardon Walker (chief operating officer), and Ronald W. Miller (Walt's son-in-law) took over the company.[9] The 75-year-old Roy would dedicate his time as chief executive officer to overseeing Walt's plans for "The Florida Project": building the Magic Kingdom in Orlando on 43 square miles (about 111 sq m) of swampland.

Unlike the city of Anaheim, which had been growing since before the Civil War, the land in Florida was largely untouched. Before the first buildings could even be started, the entire infrastructure of a modern city — from water, power, and roads to "utilidors," a unique system of tunnels to keep workers from guests' view — had to be installed.

The development of Walt Disney World's first park took four times as long as the original in Anaheim. In 1971, the same year that the 100 millionth guest[10] passed through Disneyland's front gate, the Magic Kingdom debuted on October 1, bearing more resemblances to Disneyland than Walt had originally envisioned. At the dedication ceremony, just before Roy was to address the crowd of guests, "he suddenly turned and looked around and I heard him say quietly, 'Somebody go find Mickey for me,'" John Hench recalled. "We don't have Walt anymore, and Mickey is the nearest thing to Walt that we have left.'"[11] Roy dedicated the park with Mickey at his side, and died two months later.

It would be about a decade before the Florida location would be expanded, albeit in a form quite different from the original plan. The billion-dollar EPCOT Center covered 260 acres (about 105 ha) and joined the Magic Kingdom in 1982.[12] Hench designed the focal point of EPCOT, the attraction Spaceship Earth, a 180-foot-high (nearly 55 m) geosphere inspired by the plans of R. Buckminster Fuller. Author and Disney family friend Ray Bradbury was so moved by his visits to WED Enterprises that he joined the company to write the storyline for the attraction, building the future of which he had always dreamed. EPCOT Center featured two lands: Future World, with attractions showcasing technological breakthroughs like farming on the sea floor; and World Showcase, with nine international pavilions.

East, west, home's best

The symbiotic relationship Walt established with the 1964–65 New York World's Fair became the model for new developments at the two Disney parks. Attractions designed or first built for the Orlando outpost, including Space Mountain and the Country Bear Jamboree, could be duplicated in Southern California.

John Hench, principal designer on Space Mountain, created the concept for the cone shape of the building to echo the roller coaster's expanding spiral track inside. By having the beams on the outside of the structure, the interior walls became smooth projection surfaces for fields of stars. Although Hench's plans were created as part of Tomorrowland '67, WED Enterprises had to wait until the right sponsor came along before the first roller coaster to operate in the dark would be realized, eight years later in Orlando.

The 1971 Country Bear Jamboree, on the other hand, was part of the original design for the Magic Kingdom, five *Audio-Animatronics* groups of bear musicians first conceived for Walt's shelved ski resort at Mineral King. Marc Davis remembered Walt laughing at his sketches of Trixie, Big Al, and the cast of bear characters the last time he visited the studio. It soon migrated west to Disneyland as the marquee attraction of Bear Country, the new four-acre (about two ha) land built on the former home of the Indian Village, where the "cast members" sang their hearts out for almost three decades until it made way for another ursine, Winnie the Pooh.

One attraction that originated in California but rotated between parks was the iconic Main Street Electrical Parade. The joyful spectacle of floats lit with hundreds of thousands of colorful bulbs, rolling to the futuristic electronic sounds of Jean-Jacques Perrey and Gershon Kingsley's "Baroque Hoedown," arrived at Disneyland in 1972 and ran for 24 years, with return engagements in 2001 and 2017.

In Frontierland, Mine Train Through Nature's Wonderland was exchanged for the thrilling Big Thunder Mountain Railroad in 1979, but playful homages, including the little town of Rainbow Ridge, remained. Imagineer Tony Baxter was largely responsible for the design with input from John

Hench, who encouraged the reds and earth-tone colors seen in Sedona, Arizona, and the beautifully sculpted rockwork of Bryce Canyon National Park in Utah. In 1958, *National Geographic* described that park's alien landscape as "something that looks like it was created by Walt Disney." The sprayed and sculpted stones at Disneyland were beautiful from day one, largely due to the mastery of model maker Fred Joerger, who oversaw the 104-foot-high (about 32 m) stone outcropping inspired by natural formations near Route 66 in Oatman, Arizona. His realistic rocks along the Jungle Cruise and in the grottoes of Pirates of the Caribbean were a precursor to the incredible Ornament Valley Mountain Range in Cars Land at Disney California Adventure, a separate theme park adjacent to Disneyland that opened in 2001.

Baxter also took on the challenge of redesigning the original Fantasyland, which was demolished in 1982.[13] "I remember Tony Baxter standing in the middle of all the wreckage of Walt's favorite land," said Imagineer Bruce Gordon, "standing there going, 'What have we done?' That was scary, but it came out great."[14]

In 1983, the same year that the third Disney resort opened in Tokyo, an entirely new Fantasyland debuted in Anaheim featuring stained glass and half timbers modeled on a European village. The highly

"Somebody go find Mickey for me. . . . We don't have Walt anymore, and Mickey is the nearest thing to Walt that we have left."

— Roy O. Disney

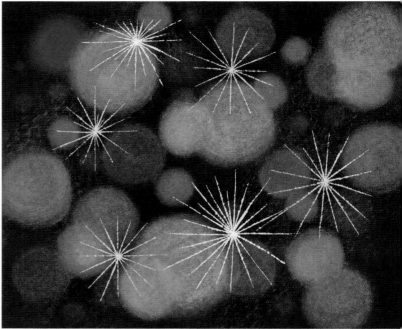

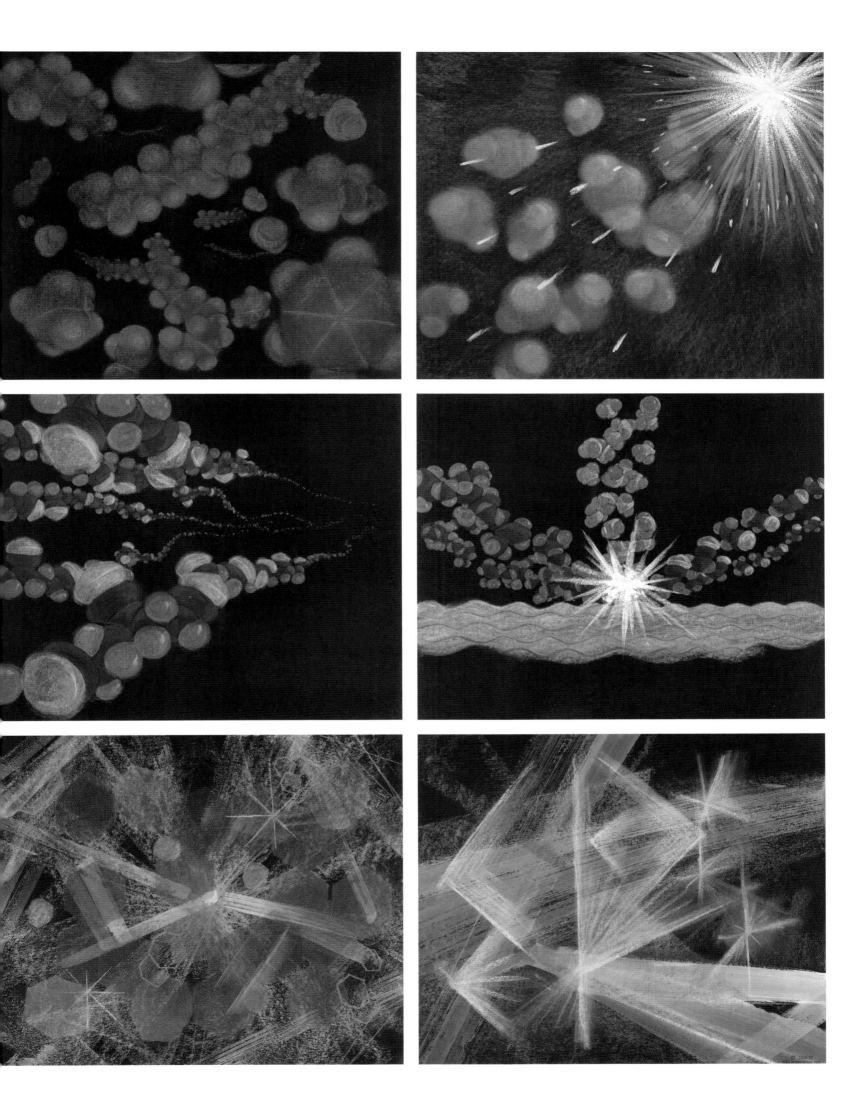

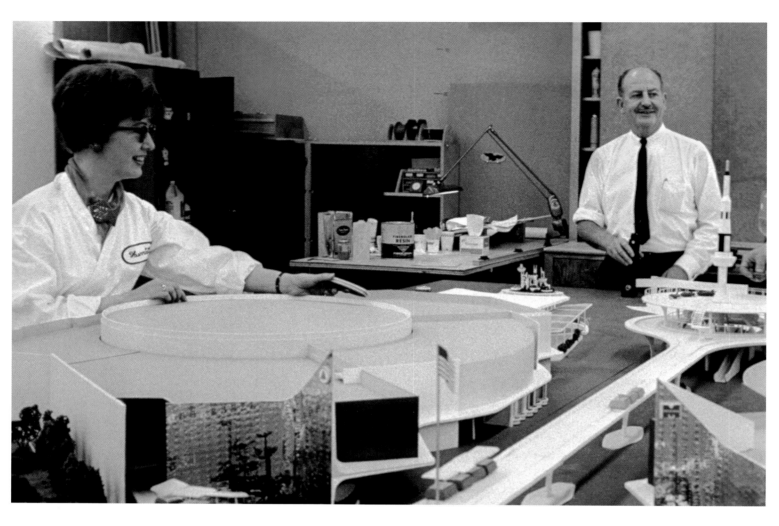

ABOVE Harriet Burns and
John Hench work on the model
for New Tomorrowland.

OPPOSITE ABOVE To keep up with the
rapid advances in technology
that rendered much of 1955's
Tomorrowland "todayland," attractions were updated or replaced:
The redesigned Rocket Jets were
elevated two stories to replace the
TWA *Moonliner* as the centerpiece
of the land.

OPPOSITE BELOW Another new attraction
in Tomorrowland slated to open
in 1967 was the PeopleMover,
a prototype rapid transportation
system of the future that would
allow guests elevated views of the
redesigned land. *Art, Herb Ryman*

detailed buildings replaced the original
medieval tent–inspired structures from
1955. An enlarged Dumbo attraction took
the place of Captain Hook's Galley, Snow
White's Adventures took a dramatic turn to
become Snow White's Scary Adventures,
and a new attraction, Pinocchio's Daring
Journey, replaced the Fantasyland Theatre.
At the revamped Fantasyland's grand opening on May 25, the drawbridge on Sleeping
Beauty Castle was lowered for the first time
since Disneyland's debut in 1955. Kathryn
Beaumont, the actress who voiced Alice in
the 1951 *Alice in Wonderland* film, returned
to record the voice of Alice for the updated
attraction. "I was 11 years old when I did
it the first time," Beaumont remembered.
"So, it was a bit difficult to get my voice to go
that high."[15]

Bear Country was renamed Critter
Country with the opening of Splash Mountain
in 1989. The attraction took the form of
an amusement-park flume ride — in which
guests drift along a canal in a hollowed-
out log — through a landscape inspired by
Disney's *Song of the South* (1946). A cast of
Audio-Animatronics critters (many repurposed from the America Sings attraction
in Tomorrowland) belt out the film's signature song, "Zip-A-Dee-Doo-Dah," before it

transitions to a log flume thrill ride for the
grand finale: a 52-foot (nearly 16 m), water-
soaked plunge through a briar patch.

The closure of America Sings was not
the only change slated for Tomorrowland.
"Originally, we were in a time fascinated
by what the future might become," said
Imagineer Tim Delaney. "Now, the focus
is to create fantasy about the future."[16]
Tomorrowland found a new science-fiction
champion when George Lucas teamed up
with director Francis Ford Coppola and the
Imagineers to create *Captain EO*, a short,
3-D musical film starring Michael Jackson.
It opened in 1986 at the 750-seat Magic Eye
Theater, but just months later an even more
immersive film/attraction hybrid debuted
when Lucas adapted *Star Wars* (1977) into the
attraction Star Tours, built inside the former
location of Adventure Thru Inner Space.
The theater was equipped with four military
flight simulators that allowed 1,600 people
an hour to fly through the galaxy with
C-3PO and R2-D2.

By the 1990s, space was at a premium
in Disneyland, and new attractions were
integrated among the classics in innovative
ways. In 1992, the same year that Disney's
fourth resort in Paris opened, "Fantasmic!"
came to Disneyland. Invisible during the

day, the show rose out of the Rivers of America each evening. In it, Mickey battled a dragon as scenes from Disney films were projected onto three mist screens amid pyrotechnical displays.

In the following year, a whole new land ballooned to life behind the berm with the opening of Mickey's Toontown, a three-dimensional cartoon environment reminiscent of the 1988 film *Who Framed Roger Rabbit*. Visitors could immerse themselves in a colorful, interactive world of rolling Jolly Trolley cars; tour the cartoony houses where Mickey, Minnie, and other lovable characters lived; or take a wacky trip through cartoon noir on Roger Rabbit's Car Toon Spin.

The movie-inspired attractions continued when the Indiana Jones Adventure opened in Adventureland on March 3, 1995. The tomb-raiding professor, introduced in *Raiders of the Lost Ark* (1981), sends fans on a journey through the Temple of the Forbidden Eye on an "enhanced-motion" transport, rollicking through the cursed ruins. Lauded by many as the most immersive attraction since the days of Walt, the scenes are inspired by the action and atmosphere of the first three Indiana Jones films, with 160,000 possible show-programming combinations.

Back in Tomorrowland, PeopleMover, Mission to Mars, and the Skyway all departed as the land underwent yet another revamp in 1998. Inspired by the 19th-century futurism of Jules Verne, the district was recast in shades of bronze, and its new centerpiece was a fresh take on the Rocket Jets, the Astro Orbitor. The rotating spaceships were to rise on the same site, but the new attraction was too heavy for a second-floor perch. It was moved out to the plaza area of Tomorrowland to become the icon at its entrance.

While Disney was opening its fifth resort in Hong Kong in 2005, back at home, creative chief Marty Sklar and Imagineers Bruce Gordon and Tony Baxter were advocating for the classic Submarine Voyage. They were successful in giving it a new lease on life in 2007 as the Finding Nemo Submarine Voyage, based on the popular Disney•Pixar film, and it continues to entertain guests today. Of the achievement, Sklar said: "I'm sure glad I didn't have to throw myself across Harbor Boulevard [to save it]," as he had threatened to do so publicly if the ride were eliminated. "I never gave up."[17] Baxter also helped another classic Disneyland fixture reopen. After a decade-long closure, the Sleeping Beauty Castle walk-through attraction was completely restored in 2008.

California, here I come

After 46 years of constantly evolving and expanding its extraordinary theme lands — to much success and fanfare — Disneyland was ready to offer something entirely different. The outdoor Downtown Disney shopping and entertainment center, the 900-plus-room Grand Californian Hotel, and a brand-new, 55-acre theme park called Disney's California Adventure opened in 2001, built on the site of Disneyland's original parking lot. (Its name was changed to Disney California Adventure Park in 2012.)

California Adventure offered a glimpse of a classic California vacation and was organized into three lands: a seaside district called Paradise Pier, a Hollywood Pictures Backlot, and the Golden State. In the press release announcing the park, Barry Braverman, the Imagineering executive producer of the park, said this of the design:

> *This wasn't to be a theme park in the traditional Disney sense.... You can stand at the park's entry plaza and see the gateway to Golden State; you can see the California Grizzly Bear icon high atop Grizzly Peak; you can see the gates to Hollywood; and you can see Paradise Pier's massive roller coaster, along with so much more.*

The Soarin' Over California attraction was an instant hit. Riders fly aboard enormous gliders on an innovative lift system that allows them to feel the wind blowing and catch the scent of pine trees, orange blossoms, and ocean surf in the air while their feet dangle in front of an 80-foot (about 24 m), half-dome-shaped screen. Another early standout was the dining area at the Pacific Wharf. Guests could watch sourdough bread, tortillas, and fortune cookies being created from scratch at Boudin Bakery, Mission Tortillas, and Lucky Fortune Cookery, respectively, and learn about the winemaking process at the Robert Mondavi Golden Vine Winery. Historic California architecture — including a mission-style train-station tower inspired by the Santa Fe Depot in San Diego and Los Angeles landmarks such as the Pantages Theatre and Bullocks Wilshire — were whimsically replicated. The park was not as thoughtfully planned as Disneyland though, and management noticed that many guests were satisfied after a single visit.

"Almost all artwork, no matter what the final form, begins with drawing because drawing is the artists' fundamental tool."

—Mary Blair

and the Seven Dwarfs premiered in 1937. The biggest addition to California Adventure was the highly detailed Route 66–themed Cars Land inspired by the 2006 film *Cars*. The roadside attractions and programmatic architecture that inspired the movie come to life here along with historic relics dotting the celebrated roadway.

In 2016, Disney realized Iger's vision for a theme park in mainland China with the opening of Shanghai Disney Resort, while a 14-acre (almost 6 ha) transformation got underway at both Disneyland in California and Disney's Hollywood Studios in Florida, as construction began on new lands inspired by George Lucas's *Star Wars* films. "We are creating a jaw-dropping new world that represents our largest single themed land expansion ever," Iger said, when making the announcement in July 2015. "These new lands at Disneyland and Walt Disney World will transport guests to a whole new *Star Wars* planet, including an epic *Star Wars* adventure that puts you in the middle of a climactic battle between the First Order and the Resistance."

Walt Disney's incredible persistence and visionary idea created a central institution in American culture. Another innovative mind, the visionary developer James Rouse, extolled Walt's unconventional park in a 1963 speech at Harvard University:

> *I hold a view that may be somewhat shocking to an audience as sophisticated as this…that the greatest piece of urban design in the United States today is Disneyland. If you think about Disneyland and think of its performance in relation to its purpose — its meaning to people more than its meaning to the process of development — you will find it the outstanding piece of urban design in the United States.*[19]

Disneyland is not just an entertainment destination that has lasted generations and has been duplicated around the world, it is a glorious symbol of a golden age that historian Alan Hess refers to as "Imperial California." Disneyland is a shared language. It is shorthand for the optimism that fueled the 20th century and continues to inspire us today. The original ideas pioneered in Anaheim have spread around the world, and the dreams of Walt Disney have influenced generations. Millions of us have visited Disneyland, but we all feel like family… Like Walt said on opening day, "Disneyland is your land." Now go out and enjoy it.

ABOVE Roy O. Disney would have Mickey Mouse at his side at many events after Walt's passing, from a press preview of the new Tomorrowland in 1967 to the dedication of Walt Disney World (above) in October 1971.

OPPOSITE All new transportation systems appeared in the new Tomorrowland, from the Goodyear PeopleMover and new Skyway gondolas to the completely rebuilt Astro-Jets, now the Rocket Jets.

This led new Disney chairman and chief executive officer Bob Iger to announce a $1.1-billion makeover[18] of the six-year-old park in 2007, with the goal of creating a more nuanced and carefully themed design, and perhaps, most importantly, create a tribute to the man who turned an orange grove in Anaheim into a worldwide phenomenon: Walt Disney. The first noticeable change was a new entrance modeled after the Pan-Pacific Auditorium, designed by Walt's old friend Welton Becket of Plummer, Wurdeman and Becket. The redesign was meant to transport visitors to the Los Angeles that Walt Disney knew in the 1920s and '30s. Replicas of Red Car trolleys run past historic landmarks. A fine-dining restaurant and members-only club resides inside the centerpiece, a spectacular recreation of the Carthay Circle Theatre, where *Snow White*

PREVIOUS When the Space Mountain complex opened in 1977, it included the video game–filled Starcade, and a performance venue called the Space Stage. Guests aboard the PeopleMover got a sneak peek inside. *Art, Clem Hall*

ABOVE At night, the future was all the more stunning in the new Tomorrowland. Guests could enjoy fireworks burst over the Matterhorn while boarding the PeopleMover or flying in the Rocket Jets.

RIGHT Space Mountain's spiral-cone shape was created by John Hench to echo the expanding coil track of the roller coaster. It was the second roller coaster in Disneyland and the first in the world to be completely enclosed. The complete darkness offers guests the thrill of hurtling through space. *Art, Chuck Ballew*

OPPOSITE By featuring the structural beams on the exterior of the Space Mountain dome, interior surfaces were left smooth, enabling projections that create the illusion of traveling through the cosmos.

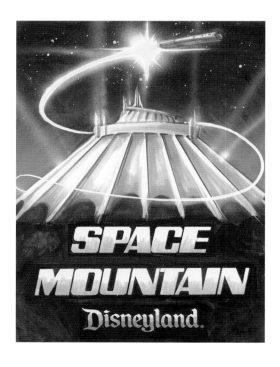

OPPOSITE **Boxing legend Muhammad Ali signed autographs in the newly renovated Tomorrowland during a visit in 1967.**

ABOVE AND RIGHT **John Hench started designing the space-inspired ride in 1965, prior to Walt Disney's death, as part of Tomorrowland '67, but the attraction was not realized until a decade later, when it first debuted at Walt Disney World. Hench recalled, "It took eleven years to find a location [at Disneyland] and a financial sponsor."** *Art, John Hench*

ABOVE AND LEFT As times changed, Tomorrowland began to look away from science and technology and embrace fantasy visions of the future for thematic inspiration. In 1986, George Lucas teamed up with director Francis Ford Coppola to bring *Captain EO* to the evolving land. The 3-D musical film, complete with immersive special effects, was shown in the Magic Eye Theater (which replaced the Space Stage) and starred superstar Michael Jackson as its titular hero. *Art, Chris Runco (above); P. Winkley (left)*

OPPOSITE Captain EO's faithful crew —Hooter, Fuzzball, the Geex, Major Domo, and Minor Domo—were puppets created by Lance Anderson and Rick Baker, who created the infamous zombies for Jackson's "Thriller" music video. *Art, Joe Rohde*

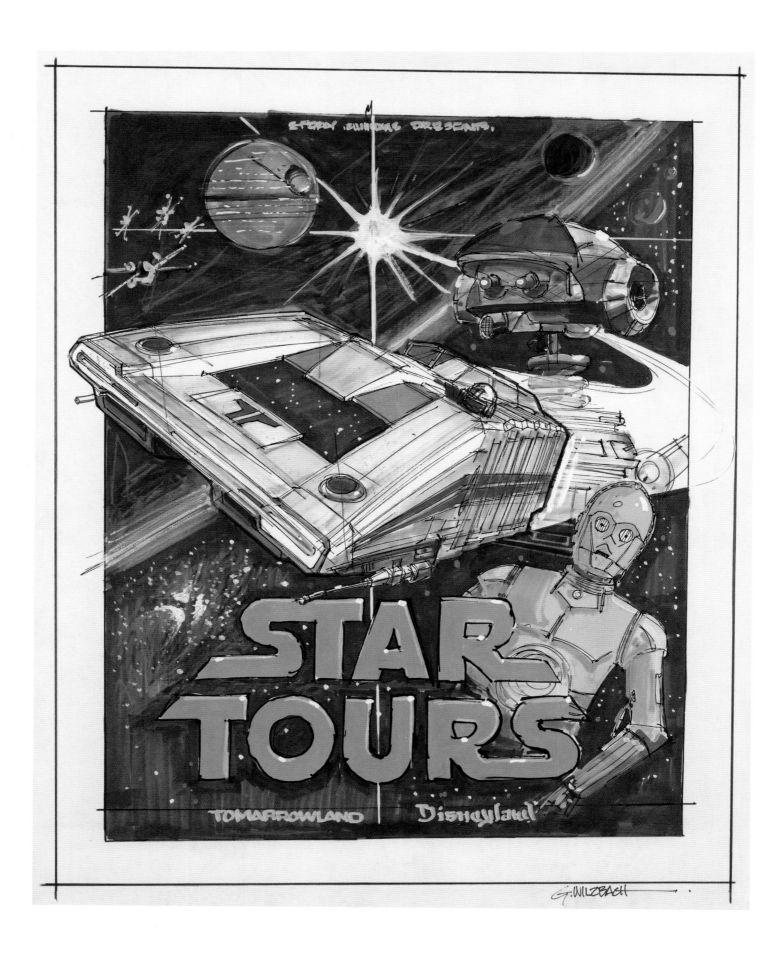

OPPOSITE **Replacing Adventure Thru Inner Space in January 1987, Star Tours invited guests to be galactic tourists on an ill-fated flight aboard a StarSpeeder 3000 to the moon of Endor. At the helm of the spacecraft was friendly pilot Rex.** *Art, Greg Wilzbach*

ABOVE **The groundbreaking interstellar attraction, inspired by George Lucas's *Star Wars* films, features four industrial flight simulators capable of sending 1,600 guests per hour across the galaxy at light speed.** *Art, John Hench*

RIGHT **Schematics of droids and other technology from the films added layers of thematic richness to the queue and environs of Star Tours.** *Art, S. Yokoyama*

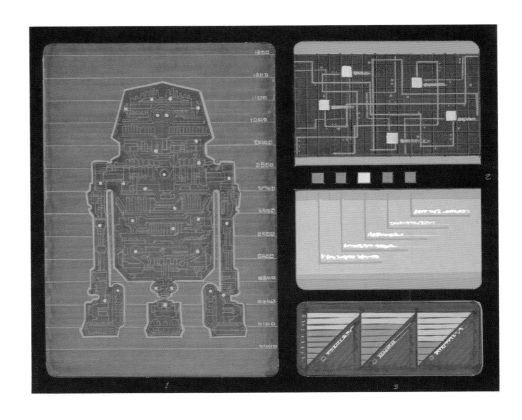

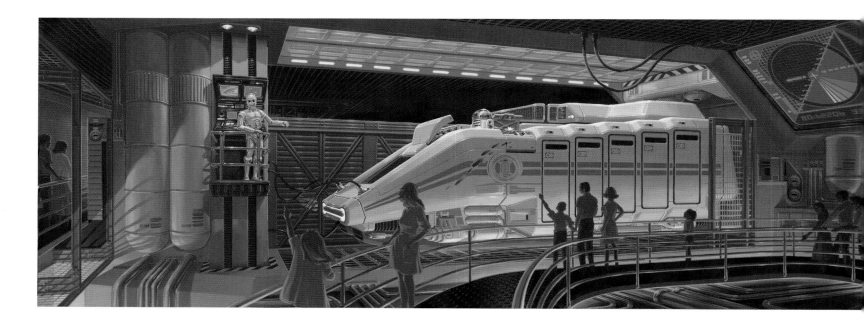

ABOVE Guests in the preshow queue of Star Tours encountered R2-D2, C-3PO, and a full-scale StarSpeeder 3000, located in the same spot previously occupied by the Mighty Microscope of Monsanto's Adventure Thru Inner Space attraction. *Art, Gil Keppler*

RIGHT The thrilling flight on the Endor Express was made possible by the integration of film, *Audio-Animatronics*, and motion-simulator technologies. *Art, Collin Campbell*

FOLLOWING *Mountain, Anaheim*, 2013. In 2006, after nearly a decade of closure, the Submarine Voyage in Tomorrowland was reopened as the Finding Nemo Submarine Voyage, featuring characters from the 2003 Disney•Pixar film and an entirely new storyline. *Photo, Thomas Struth*

"The idea was...I would like to make an action movie which is more like a Saturday matinee serial that I enjoyed as a kid but imbue it with mythological, psychological motifs."
—George Lucas

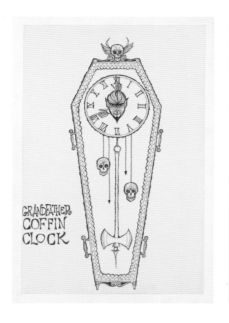

GRANDFATHER COFFIN CLOCK

THIS PAGE The Haunted Mansion went through more than a decade of design development before opening in 1969. Early concept illustrations by Rolly Crump for an unrealized Museum of the Weird influenced the ghoulishly anthropomorphic fixtures, furniture, and wallpaper found throughout the finished attraction. *Art, Rolly Crump*

ABOVE Early Disneyland concepts included unrealized plans for a haunted house to be located off to the side of Main Street, U.S.A. New Orleans Square proved to be the perfect location for an attraction of ghoulish delights that would materialize with the 1969 opening of the Haunted Mansion. *Art, Collin Campbell*

RIGHT The Haunted Mansion was in development for almost 20 years with contributions from some of Disneyland's most noted designers. Art director Ken Anderson worked closely with Walt hashing out concepts, including the ghost host, the transformation from a walk-though to a tracked conveyance, and these ghostly apparitions from 1963. "It was proven to me then that you couldn't walk through this place and be able to see and hear all the things we were planning." *Art, Ken Anderson*

ABOVE **Marc Davis brought much of the gallows humor to the characters and scenes, while Claude Coats created the attraction's sinister mood through his design of its eerie environments. This early Davis sketch imagines the gallery of creepy portraits that change to reveal the unfortunate, often humorous, fates of their subjects.** *Art, Marc Davis*

LEFT **One of the portraits in the Haunted Mansion features a woman who slowly transforms into a cat. Although guests do not see an actual ghost "materialize" until midpoint in the attraction, Davis's "changing portraits" are heavily featured in the preshow, and set the unnerving tone of the adventure ahead.** *Art, Marc Davis*

OPPOSITE **An unused changing-portrait concept featured Russian mystic monk Rasputin, who had advised Tsar Nicholas II and was murdered in 1916.** *Art, Marc Davis*

·APRIL·

·JUNE·

·SEPTEMBER·

·DECEMBER·

OPPOSITE Master illusioneer Yale Gracey developed a cross-dissolving rear-projection system that made the haunted paintings of the portrait corridor eerily transform before guests' eyes, including the memorable "April–December" portrait. Of all the haunted portraits, perhaps the most ominous is the one that all of us are anticipating. *Art, Marc Davis*

RIGHT Another unused changing-portrait concept captures the dark humor Davis brought to the attraction. *Art, Marc Davis*

BELOW Artist Ed Kohn was responsible for transforming the concept art created by Davis into the finished portraits seen in the Haunted Mansion.

BANQUET IN CLUB ROOM

© 1968 BY
WED ENTERPRISES, INC.

HAUNTED MANSION

ABOVE **The ghostly effect of the macabre merrymakers was realized through a Victorian-era illusion technique called Pepper's Ghost.**
Art, Marc Davis

LEFT **An early concept sketch imagines the iconic hitchhiking ghosts from the Haunted House finale as more cartoonish apparitions.**
Art, Marc Davis

OPPOSITE **Yale Gracey, responsible for creating the many effects that enabled the 999 happy haunts of the Haunted Mansion to materialize, poses with the Hatbox Ghost, a short-lived character from the original attic scene that was brought back in 2015.**

BELOW **Mr. Toad's Wild Ride is the only Disneyland attraction to feature the word ride in its name. With its final scene that literally transports guests to hell and back, it lives up to its moniker.** *Art, Phil Dagort*

RIGHT **An all-new dark ride attraction that replaced the Fantasyland Theater in 1983 was Pinocchio's Daring Journey, based on the 1940 film, with guests venturing into his world in a woodcarver's cart. Like other new architecture in the land, many exterior design elements of the attraction alluded to the story within. A whale-shaped weather vane is a subtle warning to riders of the imminent encounter with Monstro the Whale inside.** *Art, David Negron*

OPPOSITE BELOW **An unrealized concept for Pinocchio's Daring Journey would have had guests riding through the attraction in "wind-up" vehicles inspired by the mechanical toys featured in the 1940 animated film.** *Art, Joyce Edington*

"I remember Tony Baxter standing in the middle of all the wreckage of Walt's favorite land standing there going, 'What have we done?' That was scary, but it came out great."

—Bruce Gordon

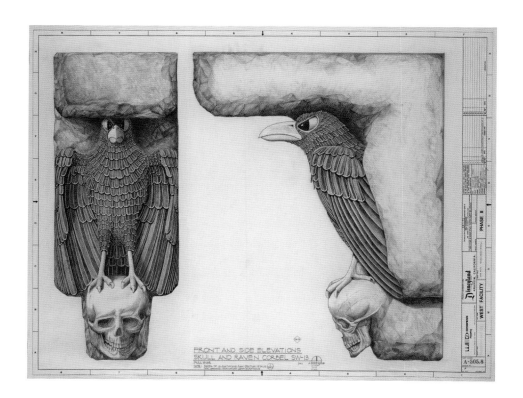

ABOVE Another welcome sight at the reopening of Fantasyland in 1983 was the elaborate new exterior for Snow White's Scary Adventures and other attractions. The medieval-tournament aesthetic of 1955 was shed in favor of fully realized facades that were evocative of the locations of the films they represent. *Art, Jacques Charvet*

LEFT The rich architectural detail of Snow White's Scary Adventures is seen in this drawing of the raven-shaped corbels that would adorn the Queen's tower, the attraction's entrance. *Art, Christopher Carradine*

OPPOSITE As part of the 1983 redesign of Fantasyland, Dumbo the Flying Elephant was enlarged and relocated to the former site of Captain Hook's Pirate Ship. Placed next to the entrance to the Casey Jr. Circus Train, the redesign offered a thematic interplay between the two Fantasyland attractions based on the 1941 animated feature *Dumbo*. *Art, David Negron (above)*

OPPOSITE AND RIGHT Originally located just behind the King Arthur Carrousel, the Mad Tea Party, with its colorful spinning cups and saucers, would be relocated to the area adjacent to the Alice in Wonderland attraction as part of the new layout of Fantasyland. *Photo, Marc Tulane; art, Kim Irvine*

BELOW The painted-flats scenes of the original fun house–style Alice in Wonderland dark ride were replaced in 1983 by large dimensional props and set pieces representing key moments of the 1951 film. Also added to the attraction was a new narration track recorded by actor Kathryn Beaumont, the original voice of Alice in the film. *Art, Marty Kline*

FOLLOWING Located behind "it's a small world" and the Fantasyland train station, Mickey's Toontown opened its gates in 1993, inviting guests into the homes of Mickey Mouse and his friends. Inspired by the 1988 film *Who Framed Roger Rabbit*, a new dark ride was added to the roster of Disneyland attractions with Roger Rabbit's Car Toon Spin. *Photo, Tim Street-Porter*

TEA PARTY
REPAINT EXISTING PROPS. ADD TEA-POTS AND SMALL DORMOUSE.

ABOVE The architectural styling of Bear Country evokes the locales of the Pacific Northwest and Adirondacks and served to differentiate the location of the new land from Frontierland and New Orleans Square. *Art, Dorothea Redmond*

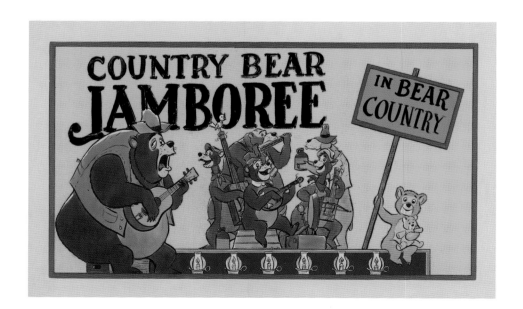

LEFT Originally planned for the unrealized Mineral King Ski Resort, the Country Bear Jamboree musical variety show was in development when Walt Disney died in 1966. *Art, Bill Justice*

OPPOSITE LEFT *Country Bear Christmas Special*, a holiday version of the show, opened in 1984 and was the first example of a Disneyland attraction receiving a holiday overlay. *Art, David Feiten*

OPPOSITE RIGHT Crocodile band the Swamp Boys serenaded guests of the sit-down Tomorrowland attraction America Sings from 1974 to 1988, before being relocated in 1989 to the log-flume attraction Splash Mountain. *Art, Marc Davis*

"THE OKEFENOKEE SWAMP BOYS"

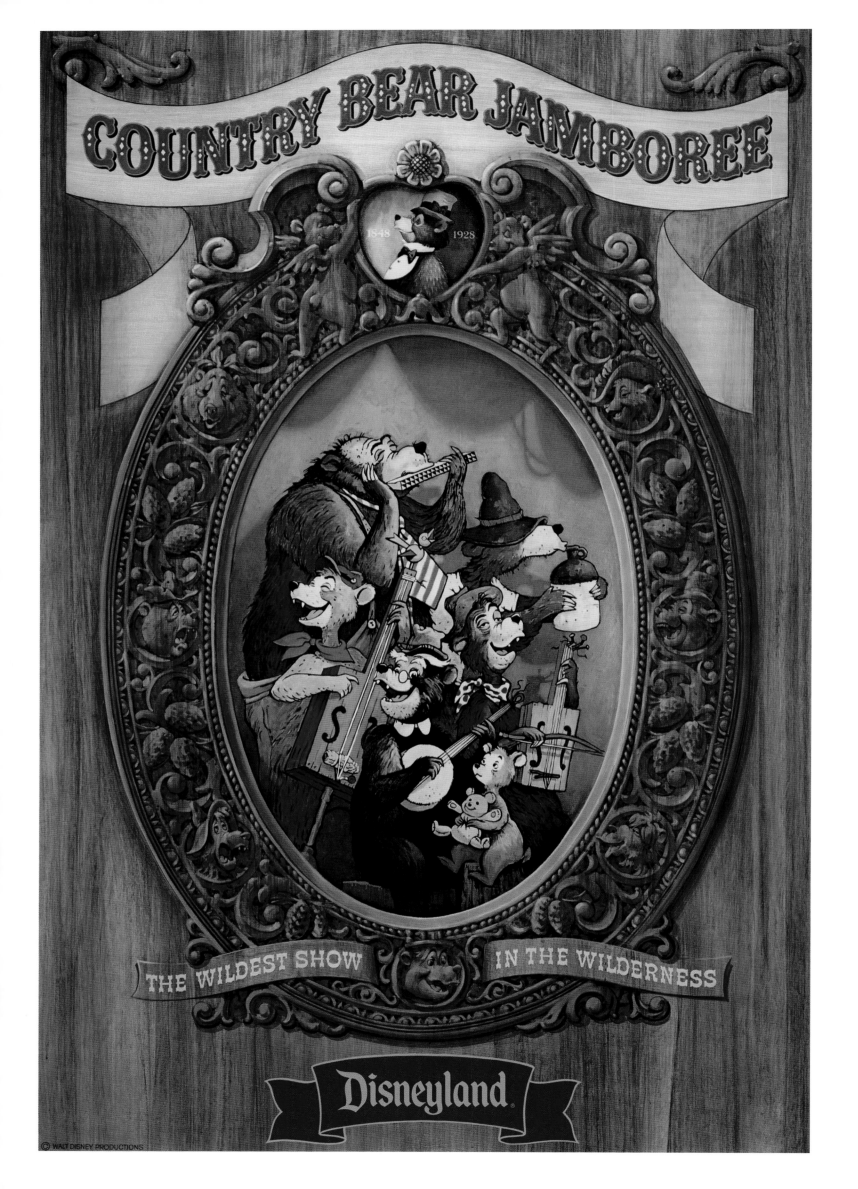

© WALT DISNEY PRODUCTIONS

ABOVE In 1979, a new mountain arrived in Frontierland as part of a thrilling new attraction, Big Thunder Mountain Railroad. With rock formations inspired by those in Bryce Canyon, Utah, and Sedona, Arizona, the ride would take guests via runaway mine train on "the wildest ride in the wilderness." *Art, Tony Baxter*

FOLLOWING While Big Thunder Mountain Railroad replaced the slower-paced Mine Train Through Nature's Wonderland, elements of the old attraction, including the miniature town of Rainbow Ridge, were integrated into the themed environment that surrounded the new rollercoaster-type attraction.

OPPOSITE Marc Davis recalled his last interaction with Walt Disney took place in 1966 as Davis was sketching the Country Bear Jamboree characters. Walt told Marc he "really had a winner here with these musical bears." Walt would die a few days later, and Davis believes it was his last good laugh. *Art, Jim Michaelson, Marc Davis, and Eddie Martinez*

"TA-TA-RA BOOM DE-AY!"

M.C. — For a history of American music!

Different costumes for different periods!

THIS SPREAD Largely designed by
Marc Davis, America Sings opened
in 1974 to replace the Carousel of
Progress show when the attraction
was relocated to Walt Disney World.
The musical variety show was
intended to coincide with America's
bicentennial and took guests on a
tour of American musical history with
acts dedicated to the Old South,
the Wild West, the Gay Nineties,
and modern times. *Art, Marc Davis;
Ray Aragon (right)*

"**Yankee Doodle remembers when, to make these songs ring true, people came from every land to mix these tunes for you. So we should all remember, as history moves along, that everything is better 'cause someone wrote a song.**"

—America Sings

PREVIOUS The Southern gospel group singing "Down by the Riverside" was among the cast of America Sings, many members of which now appear in Splash Mountain's riverboat scene.

LEFT During the musical finale of the attraction, guests pass a miniature showboat packed with animals belting out "Zip-A-Dee-Doo-Dah." *Art, Collin Campbell*

BELOW When the musical show ended its run at the rotating theater in Tomorrowland in 1988, many of its colorful *Audio-Animatronics* animal singers were recast in the showboat finale of Splash Mountain.

THIS SPREAD **Splash Mountain opened in Critter Country in 1989, inspired by the 1946 musical feature** Song of the South. **Guests follow Brer Rabbit, Brer Bear, and Brer Fox before getting thrown into the briar patch, a plunge of 52 feet (nearly 16 m) down Chick-A-Pin Hill.** Art, John Stone (top row); Guy Vasilovich (above); Sam McKim (right)

INDIANA JONES RIDE MARQUEE   6·24·93

If adventure
has a place…

INDIANA JONES

COMING SOON TO ADVENTURELAND

THIS SPREAD **In 1995, another movie-inspired attraction came to Disneyland. Based on the popular George Lucas films, Indiana Jones Adventure opened in Adventureland and allowed guests to venture deep into the cursed Temple of the Forbidden Eye in search of riches,** **youth, or boundless knowledge. Like Star Tours, things quickly take a wrong turn and guests are sent careening through the booby-trapped temple searching for Indiana Jones and a way out.** *Art, Gil Keppler (opposite); Nina Rae Vaughn (above)*

On the banner: INDY EXPEDITION LEAVING SOON

"*Originally, we were in a time fascinated by what the future might become. Now, the focus is to create fantasy about the future.*"

—Tim Delaney

ABOVE As guests enter the Temple of the Forbidden Eye, a computer-controlled show system manages everything from lighting and scrim effects to special effects, offering nearly 160,000 possible show-programming combinations. *Art, Chuck Ballew*

RIGHT The famous rolling-boulder scene from the 1981 film *Raiders of the Lost Ark* inspired the Indiana Jones Adventure finale. An early concept board imagined the use of a pivoting arm to enable the effect. In the realized attraction, the massive stone ball "rolls" in place; the feeling of the enhanced-motion ride vehicle is heightened by the room itself moving around the guests. *Art, Chuck Ballew*

PREVIOUS *Ride, Anaheim*, 2013. With its rich theming and innovative use of new technologies, Indiana Jones Adventure took "the concept of amusement park attraction to a new level," according to the *Los Angeles Times*. Numerous available variations make it possible "to go through the ride dozens of times without ever having the exact same experience." *Photo, Thomas Struth*

ABOVE Disney's California Adventure opened February 2001 on the site of Disneyland's original parking lot. The entirely new theme park packed the thrill and romance of the 31ˢᵗ state into 55 acres and featured three themed lands: Paradise Pier, Hollywood Pictures Backlot, and Golden State. *Photo, David McNew*

OPPOSITE A $1.1-billion-dollar expansion and makeover of California Adventure was announced in 2007. Its biggest addition was the Route 66–themed Cars Land, which immerses guests in the world of the 2006 animated film *Cars*. Flo's V8 Café offers diners a chance to relive a moment of neon-trimmed roadside Americana that references the same span of time that Main Street, U.S.A., did when Disneyland first opened. *Photo, Jorge Villalba*

"Virtual Reality is basically nothing new. We have been creating Virtual Reality around here for more than forty years."

—John Hench

"[Disneyland] will transport guests to a whole new Star Wars planet, including an epic Star Wars adventure that puts you in the middle of a climactic battle between the First Order and the Resistance."

—Bob Iger

LEFT **Opened in 2019, the highly anticipated** *Star Wars*: **Galaxy's Edge marked the largest expansion in the history of the park. In addition to having familiar characters and such iconic spacecraft as X-wing fighters, it has an exotic marketplace that transports visitors to a galaxy far, far away, as seen in this conceptual artwork.** *Art, Erik Tiemens and Khang Le*

BELOW AND FOLLOWING **As shown in early conceptual renderings,** *Star Wars* **fans will have the opportunity to fly one of the most famous ships in the galaxy, the Millennium Falcon; explore a Star Destroyer; and see many familiar faces, including BB-8 and Chewbacca, in the new land.** *Art, Richard Lim (below); Greg Pro, Erik Tiemens, and Nick Gindraux (following)*

Endnotes

Introduction

1 „Disneyland's first kids: These two were the first boy, girl in the gate in 1955" by Joseph Pimentel, November 18, 2015, https://www.ocregister.com/2015/11/18/video-disneylands-first-kids-these-two-were-the-first-boy-girl-in-the-gate-in-1955/.

Southern California's Happiest Export

1 Walt Disney interview with Fletcher Markle, September 25, 1963. Quoted in Jim Korkis, "Fifteen Inspirations for Disneyland—Part One," MousePlanet, July 8, 2015. https://www.mouseplanet.com/11074/Fifteen_Inspirations_for_Disneyland_Part_One.

2 M. Broggie, Walt Disney's Railroad Story: The Small-Scale Fascination That Led to A Full-Scale Kingdom (Pasadena, CA: Pentrex Media Group, 1998), 33.

3 "Picturing the Walt Disney Museum," The Walt Disney Family Museum, June 21, 2016, http://walt-disney.org/walt-disney#his-stories.

4 C.E. Davis, Jr., "Honors for Mr. Lincoln," Los Angeles Times, March 1, 1965, 30.

5 Neal Gabler, Walt Disney: The Triumph of the American Imagination (New York: Knopf, 2007), 484.

6 "Origins of the Henry Ford," The Henry Ford, https://www.thehenryford.org/collections-and-research/digital-resources/popular-topics/origins-of-thf.

7 Neal Gabler, Walt Disney: The Triumph of the American Imagination (New York: Knopf, 2007), 492.

8 Karal Ann Marling, Designing Disney's Theme Parks: the Architecture of Reassurance. (Montreal: Centre canadien d'architecture, 1997), 43.

9 Neal Gabler, Walt Disney: The Triumph of the American Imagination (New York: Knopf, 2007), 485.

10 Ibid., 490.

11 Katherine Barrett and Richard Greene, Inside the Dream: The Personal Story of Walt Disney (New York: Disney Editions, 2001), 106.

12 Ibid., 105.

13 Alan Hess, Googie: Fifties Coffee Shop Architecture (San Francisco, CA: Chronicle Books, 1986), 15.

14 Karal Ann Marling, Designing Disney's Theme Parks: the Architecture of Reassurance. (Montreal: Centre canadien d'architecture, 1997), 43.

15 Ibid., 45.

16 Ibid.

Additional Citations

p. 25 Reference to Walt at Children's Fairyland: Hank Pellissier, "Children's Fairyland," New York Times, February 5, 2011.

p. 28 Reference to restaurant buildings: George Geary, L.A.'s Legendary Restaurants: Celebrating the Famous Places Where Hollywood Ate, Drank, and Played (Solana Beach, CA: Santa Monica Press, 2016), 45, 127.

p. 28 Reference to Clifton's Cafeteria: Andrew Meieran, email to Chris Nichols, January 26, 2018.

Welcome to Disneyland

1 "Disney Reports Profit for Half," Los Angeles Times, May 22, 1951.

2 Quoted in Burbank Daily Review, March 27, 1962.

Karal Ann Marling, Designing Disney's Theme Parks: the Architecture of Reassurance (Montreal: Centre canadien d'architecture, 1997), 45.

3 "Disney has $25,250,000 TV Future, Sez Broker," Variety, March 28, 1951, 5.

4 Karal Ann Marling and Donna R. Braden, Behind the Magic: 50 Years of Disneyland. (Dearborn, Mich: The Henry Ford, 2005), 70.

5 Ibid., 55.

6 Sam Gennawey, Walt and The Promise of Progress City (Pike Road, AL: Ayefour, 2011), 109.

7 Neal Gabler, Walt Disney: The Triumph of the American Imagination (New York: Knopf, 2007), 493.

8 C.E. Davis, Jr., "Honors for Mr. Lincoln," Los Angeles Times, March 1, 1965, 30.

9 Sam Gennawey, Walt and The Promise of Progress City (Pike Road, AL: Ayefour, 2011), 109.

10 Ibid.

11 Walt Disney, as recalled by Marty Sklar in Dream It! Do It!: My Half-Century Creating Disney's Magic Kingdoms (New York: Disney Editions, 2013), 32.

12 Sam Gennawey, Walt and The Promise of Progress City (Pike Road, AL: Ayefour, 2011), 109.

13 S. Vernon, "Reflections on a Man and His Dream," Los Angeles Times, January 20, 1980, A12.

14 Neal Gabler, Walt Disney: The Triumph of the American Imagination (New York: Knopf, 2007), 495.

15 Ibid., 496.

16 Sam Gennawey, Walt and The Promise of Progress City (Pike Road, AL: Ayefour, 2011), 112.

17 Ibid., 115.

18 Katherine Barrett and Richard Greene, Inside the Dream: The Personal Story of Walt Disney (New York: Disney Editions, 2001), 108.

19 Sam Gennawey, Walt and The Promise of Progress City (Pike Road, AL: Ayefour, 2011), 131.

20 Karal Ann Marling, Designing Disney's Theme Parks: the Architecture of Reassurance (Montreal: Centre canadien d'architecture, 1997), 14.

21 Rolly Crump interview with Chris Nichols, 2016.

22 Sam Gennawey, Walt and The Promise of Progress City (Pike Road, AL: Ayefour, 2011), 120.

23 Ibid., 118.

24 Ibid.

25 Neal Gabler, Walt Disney: The Triumph of the American Imagination (New York: Knopf, 2007), 508.

26 Ibid.

27 "Disney Plans Copter Service to Disneyland," Los Angeles Times, July 6, 1954, 1.

28 Quote from "A Walk in Walt's Footsteps" Tour, Disneyland.

29 Sam Gennawey, Walt and The Promise of Progress City (Pike Road, AL: Ayefour, 2011), 115.

30 Walt Disney Productions, Disneyland: The First Thirty Years (Walt Disney Productions, 1985), 20.

31 Barrett, Katherine, and Richard Greene, Inside the dream: the personal story of Walt Disney. (New York: Disney Editions, 2001), 107.

32 Bob Gurr, Design: Just For Fun (Riverside, CA: Ape Pen Publishing & Gurr Designs, 2012), 41.

33 Robert R. Reynolds, Roller Coasters, Flumes & Flying Saucers: The Story of Ed Morgan & Karl Bacon, Ride Inventors of the Modern Amusement Parks (Jupiter, FL: Northern Lights Pub, 1999), 47.

34 Dave Smith, Disney A to Z: the Official Encyclopedia (New York: Hyperion, 1996), 133.

35 The Arrow team went to great efforts to keep Dumbo the Flying Elephant running on opening day before they were forced to put the attraction on hiatus for repairs.

36 Robert R. Reynolds, Roller Coasters, Flumes & Flying Saucers: The Story of Ed Morgan & Karl Bacon, Ride Inventors of the Modern Amusement Parks (Jupiter, FL: Northern Lights Pub, 1999).

37 Ibid.

38 Marty Sklar, Ray Bradbury, and Richard M. Sherman, Dream it! Do It!: My Half-Century Creating Disney's Magic Kingdoms (New York: Disney Editions, 2013), 74.

39 Ibid.

40 Ibid.

41 Ibid.

42 Bob Gurr interview with Chris Nichols, 2016.

43 "First 100 Units of Hotel Ready at Disneyland," Los Angeles Times, October 2, 1955, 1.

44 "Major Hotel in Disneyland Area Nearing Completion," Los Angeles Times, June 10, 1956, 1.

Additional Citations

p. 37 "Herbie, this is my dream…": Todd James Pierce, Three Years in Wonderland: The Disney Brothers, C.V. Wood, and the Making of the Great American Theme Park (Jackson, MS: University Press of Mississippi, 2016), 65.

p. 39 "Walt spent months…": Karal Ann Marling and Donna R. Braden, Behind the Magic: 50 Years of Disneyland (Dearborn, MI: The Henry Ford, 2005), 55.

p. 39 "Roy's financial and managerial expertise…": Roy E. Disney, "Setting the Record Straight on Roy O. Disney's Role," Los Angeles Times, May 28, 1995.

p. 42 Reference to Renié Conley: Jay Jorgensen and Donald L. Scoggins, Creating the Illusion: A Fashionable History of Hollywood Costume Designers (Philadelphia: Running Press, 2015), 100.

p. 45 "I want you to work on Disneyland…": Steven Watts, The Magic Kingdom: Walt Disney and the American Way of Life (Columbia, MO: University of Missouri, 1977), 435.

p. 45 "I want a hub at the end…": M. Broggie, Walt Disney's Railroad Story: The Small-Scale Fascination That Led to A Full-Scale Kingdom (Pasadena, CA: Pentrex Media Group, 1998), 208.

p. 49 "When you go to Disneyland there is no horizon…": John Hench interview with Jim Hill, 1996. "In his own words, John Hench looks back over his career at Disney," Jim Hill Media, February 8, 2004, http://jimhillmedia.com/alumni1/b/alain_littaye/archive/2004/02/09/1562.aspx.

p. 51 "The time you spend in this carefree kingdom…": Randy Bright, Disneyland: Inside Story (New York: Abrams, 1987), 81.

Main Street, U.S.A.

1 Walt Disney Productions, Disneyland: The First Thirty Years (Walt Disney Productions, 1985), 15.

2 Kelly Comras, Ruth Shellhorn (Athens, GA: University of Georgia Press, 2016), 117.

3 Sam Gennawey, *Walt and The Promise of Progress City* (Pike Road, AL: Ayefour, 2011), 79.

4 S. Vernon, "Reflections on a Man and His Dream," *Los Angeles Times*, January 20, 1980, A12.

5 Neal Gabler, *Walt Disney: The Triumph of the American Imagination* (New York: Knopf, 2007), 495.

6 Sam Gennawey, *Walt and The Promise of Progress City* (Pike Road, AL: Ayefour, 2011), 132.

7 John Hench and Peggy Van Pelt, *Designing Disney: Imagineering and the Art of the Show* (New York: Disney Editions, 2003), 69.

8 Karal Ann Marling, *Designing Disney's Theme Parks: the Architecture of Reassurance* (Montreal: Centre canadien d'architecture, 1997), 63.

9 Walt Disney, "The Disneyland Story," *Walt Disney's Wonderful World of Color*, directed by Robert Florey and Wilfred Jackson, October 1954.

10 John Hench and Peggy Van Pelt, *Designing Disney: Imagineering and the Art of the Show* (New York: Disney Editions, 2003), 79.

11 Ibid., 78.

12 "Dream Comes True in Orange Grove," *Los Angeles Times*, July 17, 1955, 2.

13 Disneyland, "Main Street," advertisement, *Los Angeles Times*, July 15, 1955.

14 Quote from C.V. Wood interview with Gregory Brown, June 14, 1977 referenced in Todd James Pierce, *Three Years in Wonderland: The Disney Brothers, C.V. Wood, and the Making of The Great American Theme Park* (Jackson, MI: University Press of Mississippi, 2016), 181.

15 John Hench and Peggy Van Pelt, *Designing Disney: Imagineering and the Art of the Show* (New York: Disney Editions, 2003), 78.

16 Ibid., 29.

17 Ibid.

18 Beth Dunlop, *Building A Dream: The Art of Disney Architecture* (New York: Abrams, 1996), 26.

19 Sam Gennawey, *Walt and The Promise of Progress City* (Pike Road, AL: Ayefour, 2011), 127.

20 Disneyland, "Main Street," advertisement, *Los Angeles Times*, July 15, 1955.

21 Neal Gabler, *Walt Disney: The Triumph of the American Imagination* (New York: Knopf, 2007), 475.

22 Bob Gurr, *Design: Just For Fun* (Riverside, CA: Ape Pen Publishing & Gurr Designs, 2012), 42.

23 Ibid., 68.

Additional Citations

p. 63 "Bank of America operated…": Neal Gabler, *Walt Disney: The Triumph of the American Imagination* (New York: Knopf, 2007), 508.

p. 74 Reference to balloon sales: Jim Korkis, "The Story of the Mickey Mouse Helium Balloons, Part One," MousePlanet, December 26, 2013, https://www.mouseplanet.com/10554/The_Story_of_the_Mickey_Mouse_Helium_Balloons_Part_One.

p. 75 "I wanted something alive…": Walt Disney Productions, *Disneyland: The First Quarter Century* (Walt Disney Productions, 1979), 108.

Adventureland

1 Walt Disney Productions, *Disneyland: The First Thirty Years* (Walt Disney Productions, 1985), 16.

2 Robert De Roos, "The Magic Worlds of Walt Disney," *National Geographic*, Vol. 124, No. 2, August 1963, 191.

3 Neal Gabler, *Walt Disney: The Triumph of the American Imagination* (New York: Knopf, 2007), 445.

4 Walt Disney, "Educational Values in Factual Nature Pictures," *Educational Horizons 33*, No. 2, 1954, 82, http://www.jstor.org/stable/42922993.

5 Bob Gurr, *Design: Just For Fun* (Riverside, CA: Ape Pen Publishing & Gurr Designs, 2012), 45.

6 "Sound Effects Add Realism to Disneyland," *Radio and Television News*, 1956, 52.

7 *Disney News*, Vol. 2, No. 4, 1967, 4.

8 Rolly Crump interview with Chris Nichols, 2016.

9 Rolly Crump, *It's Kind of A Cute Story* (Baltimore: Bamboo Forest Publishing, 2012), 57.

10 Ibid., 59.

11 Richard M. Sherman interview with Chris Nichols, 2016.

12 Rolly Crump, *It's Kind of A Cute Story* (Baltimore: Bamboo Forest Publishing, 2012), 60.

13 Ibid., 61.

14 Ibid., 62.

Frontierland

1 Dave Smith, *Disney A to Z: the Official Encyclopedia* (New York: Hyperion, 1996), 118.

2 C. Smith, "Thousands of Crockett Fans Cheer Bowl's Disney night," *Los Angeles Times*, July 15, 1955.

3 Marty Sklar, Ray Bradbury, and Richard M. Sherman, *Dream it! Do It!: My Half-Century Creating Disney's Magic Kingdoms* (New York: Disney Editions, 2013), 95.

4 "Frontierland," *Los Angeles Times*, July 15, 1955, 4-d20.

5 Ibid.

6 Ibid.

7 Ibid.

8 Quote from a promotional TV spot Walt Disney recorded for National Wildlife Week, 1966 in Walt Disney and Dave Smith, *The Quotable Walt Disney* (New York: Disney Editions, 2001), 185.

9 Bennett Cerf, "Mouse-made genius," *Los Angeles Times*, April 15, 1956, O4.

10 Edwin Schallert, "Disney Spending $2,000,000 on New Dreams for Playland, Tom Sawyer Island Among Improvements," *Los Angeles Times*, May 13, 1956, 2.

11 Bob Gurr, "1956 Disneyland Animals Before Animatronics," MiceChat, April 2, 2014, http://micechat.com/62890-design-times-28-1956-disneyland-animals-animatronics/.

12 Walt Disney, *Walt Disney's Guide to Disneyland*, 3rd edition, (Walt Disney Productions, 1958), 14.

Additional Citations

p. 121 Reference to color of cars: Bruce Gordon and Tim O'Day, *Disneyland: Then, Now, and Forever* (New York: Disney Editions, 2006), 74.

Fantasyland

1 Karal Ann Marling, *Designing Disney's Theme Parks: the Architecture of Reassurance* (Montreal: Centre canadien d'architecture, 1997), 70.

2 Walt Disney Productions, *Disneyland: The First Thirty Years* (Walt Disney Productions, 1985), 16.

3 Bob Gurr interview with Chris Nichols, 2016.

4 Robert R. Reynolds, *Roller Coasters, Flumes & Flying Saucers: The Story of Ed Morgan & Karl Bacon, Ride Inventors of the Modern Amusement Parks* (Jupiter, FL: Northern Lights Pub, 1999), 54.

5 Ibid., 47.

6 Bob Gurr, *Design: Just For Fun* (Riverside, CA: Ape Pen Publishing & Gurr Designs, 2012), 45.

7 Ibid., 53.

8 "Disney Legends: Roy Williams," D23. The Official Disney Fan Club. https://d23.com/walt-disney-legend/roy-williams/.

9 J.L. Scott, "Circus to Come to Disneyland," *Los Angeles Times*, November 20, 1955.

10 Bob Gurr, *Design: Just For Fun* (Riverside, CA: Ape Pen Publishing & Gurr Designs, 2012), 47.

11 Ibid., 64.

12 Robert R. Reynolds, *Roller Coasters, Flumes & Flying Saucers: The Story of Ed Morgan & Karl Bacon, Ride Inventors of the Modern Amusement Parks* (Jupiter, FL: Northern Lights Pub, 1999), 70.

13 Ibid.

14 Bob Gurr, *Design: Just For Fun* (Riverside, CA: Ape Pen Publishing & Gurr Designs, 2012), 63.

15 Robert R. Reynolds, *Roller Coasters, Flumes & Flying Saucers: The Story of Ed Morgan & Karl Bacon, Ride Inventors of the Modern Amusement Parks* (Jupiter, FL: Northern Lights Pub, 1999), 70.

16 Ibid., 69.

17 Ibid., 72.

18 Marty Sklar, Ray Bradbury, and Richard M. Sherman, *Dream it! Do It!: My Half-Century Creating Disney's Magic Kingdoms* (New York: Disney Editions, 2013), 93.

19 Walt Disney and Dave Smith, *The Quotable Walt Disney* (New York: Disney Editions, 2001, 249.

Additional Citations

p. 134 Reference to Skyway gondola: Bruce Gordon and Tim O'Day, *Disneyland: Then, Now, and Forever* (New York: Disney Editions, 2006), 113.

p. 146 Reference to Matterhorn climbers: Sarah Tully and Mark Eades, "Climbers Return to Disneyland's Matterhorn," *Orange County Register*, June 27, 2012.

p. 161 "We ordered all these brooms…" : Jeff Kurtti, *Walt Disney's Imagineering Legends and the Genesis of the Disney Theme Park*, (New York: Disney Publishing, 2008), 85.

p. 162 "We had to find the right degree of exaggeration…": John Hench and Peggy Van Pelt, *Designing Disney: Imagineering and the Art of the Show* (New York: Disney Editions, 2003).

p. 173 "A great poster sells its story…": Daniel Handke, Vanessa Hunt and Tony Baxter, *Poster Art of Disney Parks* (New York: Disney Editions, 2012), 5.

Tomorrowland

1 John Hench and Peggy Van Pelt, *Designing Disney: Imagineering and the Art of the Show* (New York: Disney Editions, 2003), 53.

2 H. Makemson, *Media, NASA, and America's Quest For The Moon* (New York: Peter Lang, 2009), 15.

3 Walt Disney in "Tomorrowland Promise of Things to Come."

4 Lisa Scanlon, "The House of the Future That Wasn't," *MIT Technology Review*, January 1, 2005.

5 "House with a Bounce," *Monsanto Magazine*, March 1968, 22. Monsanto Company Records (WUA00131), Washington University Archives

6 Bob Gurr, *Design: Just For Fun* (Riverside, CA: Ape Pen Publishing & Gurr Designs, 2012), 21.

7 Walt Disney, "There's Always Something New," *Los Angeles Times*, July 14, 1959.

8 Leslie Earnest, "Disneyland Scuttling Submarine Fleet," *Los Angeles Times*, July 30, 1998.

9   John Hench and Peggy Van Pelt, *Designing Disney: Imagineering and the Art of the Show* (New York: Disney Editions, 2003), 41.

10 Bob Gurr, *Design: Just For Fun* (Riverside, CA: Ape Pen Publishing & Gurr Designs, 2012), 59.

Additional Citations

p. 193 "Walt appreciated creativity…": Daniel Handke, Vanessa Hunt, and Tony Baxter, *Poster Art of Disney Parks* (New York: Disney Editions, 2012), 96.

p. 194 "If it moves on wheels at Disneyland…": Bob Gurr interview with Chris Nichols, 2016.

p. 205 "A pleasure to watch in action": John Hench and Peggy Van Pelt, *Designing Disney: Imagineering and the Art of the Show* (New York: Disney Editions, 2003), 26.

Walt Dreams Even Bigger

1   Marty Sklar, Ray Bradbury, and Richard M. Sherman, *Dream it! Do It!: My Half-Century Creating Disney's Magic Kingdoms* (New York: Disney Editions, 2013), 52.

2   Bill Cotter, "1961 Concept Art of the Unisphere," The World's Fair Community, July 30, 2016. www.worldsfaircommunity.org/topic/15540-1961-concept-art-of-the-unisphere/.

3   Quote from Marty Sklar in Robert Niles, "11 Things You Might Not Have Known About Disney and the 1964 New York World's Fair," Theme Park Insider, November 19, 2014. http://www.themeparkinsider.com/flume/201411/4302/.

4   Bill Cotter, "1961 Concept Art of the Unisphere." *The World's Fair Community*, 30 July 2016. www.worldsfaircommunity.org/topic/15540-1961-concept-art-of-the-unisphere/.

5   Quote from Walt Disney in "Disney Goes to the Fair," *Walt Disney's Wonderful World of Color*, May 17, 1964.

6   Bob Gurr, *Design: Just For Fun* (Riverside, CA: Ape Pen Publishing & Gurr Designs, 2012), 87.

7   Ray Bradbury, "The Machine-Tooled Happyland." *Holiday*, October 1965.

8   Brady Black, "Disney Master of Fantasy" *Cincinnati Pictorial Enquirer*, February 20, 1966, 24.

9   Richard M. Sherman interview with Chris Nichols, 2016.

10 Ibid.

11 Ibid.

12 Walt Disney, Rex Allen, Paul Frees, Richard M. Sherman, and Daws Butler, *Walt Disney and the 1964 World's Fair* (Burbank, CA: Walt Disney Records, 2009).

13 Rolly Crump interview with Chris Nichols, 2016.

14 Richard M. Sherman interview with Chris Nichols, 2016.

15 *Walt Disney Treasures — Tomorrow Land: Disney in Space and Beyond*, directed by Ward Kimball, Hamilton Luske, Jeff Kurtti (2004; Walt Disney Studios Home Entertainment), DVD.

16 Barry Bearack, "Florida's Epcot Center Will Combine Two Theme Parks," *Los Angeles Times*, August 27, 1982.

17 Mike Bonifer and Cardon Walker, "Disney Family Album #17–Marc Davis," Mica Productions, Walt Disney Company, 1985.

18 Interview with Diane Disney Miller by Jim Garber and Bob Garner in "Disneyland: Secrets, Stories, and Magic of the Happiest Place on Earth," 2007.

19 Joseph Titizian, "Anniversary Day," Walt Disney Family Museum, October 1, 2011, http://waltdisney.org/blog/anniversary-day.

20 Interview with X Atencio by Jim Garber and Bob Garner in "Disneyland: Secrets, Stories, and Magic of the Happiest Place on Earth," 2007.

21 "Colleagues, Admirers Mourn Passing of Famous Showman," *Los Angeles Times*, December 16, 1966, 3.

22 Ibid.

Additional Citations

p. 216 Reference to Marty Sklar and New York World's Fair: "Imagineering 60 Years of Disneyland: Panel 1 — Working With Walt." Panel, D23 Expo, Anaheim, CA, August 14, 2015.

p. 219 Reference to *Our Town*: Alyssa Carnaham, "Look Closer: 1964 New York World's Fair," Walt Disney Family Museum, June 26, 2012. waltdisney.org/blog/look-closer-1964-new-york-worlds-fair.

p. 220 "There must be some way…": Jim Korkis, "Great Moments with Mr. Lincoln and Mr. Disney," MousePlanet, September 28, 2016, www.mouseplanet.com/11554/Great_Moments_With_Mr_Lincoln_and_Mr_Disney.

p. 225 "People don't walk out of the attraction…": *Walt Disney Imagineering: A Behind the Dreams Look at Making the Magic Real* (New York: Hyperion, 1996), 130.

p. 226 "It was a powerful package…": Jeff Kurtti and Bruce Gordon, *Art of Disneyland* (New York: Disney Editions, 2005), 92.

p. 230 "The key to the success…": *Walt Disney Imagineering: A Behind the Dreams Look at Making the Magic Real* (New York: Hyperion, 1996), 51.

p. 231 "Usually I begin making little doodle sketches…": *The Ceramic Mural: Modern Use of An Ancient Art*, filmed by Norman Wright Productions, Walt Disney Productions, 1967.

p. 231 "Walt was a marvelous boss…": "Imagineering 60 Years of Disneyland: Panel 2 — Continuing The Legacy." Panel, D23 Expo, Anaheim, CA, August 14, 2015.

p. 234 "All the great art directors…": Marty Sklar quoted in "Dorothea Redmond," D23. The Official Disney Fan Club, d23.com/walt-disney-legend/dorothea-redmond.

p. 237 "From the lacy iron grillwork…": Jeff Kurtti and Bruce Gordon, *Art of Disneyland* (New York: Disney Editions, 2005), 50.

p. 239 Reference to "A Pirate's Life": Werner Weiss, "Pirates Arcade Museum," Yesterland. August 6, 2016.

p. 241 "They were having fun…": Jason Surrell, *Pirates of the Caribbean: From the Magic Kingdom to the Movies* (New York: Disney Editions, 2007), 32.

p. 246 "Think of it this way…": Ibid., 30.

p. 247 "Pirates of the Caribbean literally saved Disneyland…": Ibid., 51.

Disneyland Is Your Land

1   Walt Disney Productions Annual Report, 1967, 1.

2   "Dick Nunis on New York World's Fair, Plans for Walt Disney World," Disneyana Fan Club luncheon, July 16, 2015. Youtube, 8:05. Posted July 2015. https://www.youtube.com/watch?v=f2wkU9adp54&feature=youtu.be&t=2m36s.

3   Arelo Sederberg, "Disney Annual Meeting Gets the Word: No Merger Or Sale." *Los Angeles Times*, February 8, 1967.

4   Ibid.

5   Walt Disney Productions, *Disneyland: The First Thirty Years* (Walt Disney Productions, 1985), 84.

6   John Hench and Peggy Van Pelt, *Designing Disney: Imagineering and the Art of the Show* (New York: Disney Editions, 2003), 69.

7   Kate Mather, "Just Tell 'Em that Walt Sent You; Disneyland's Club 33 Seeks New Members — for $25,000 Plus Dues of $10,000 A Year," *Los Angeles Times*, May 8, 2012.

8   "Roy Disney Relinquishes Post of President, Remains Chairman," *Los Angeles Times*, November 15, 1968.

9   W. Warga, "A New Troika Heads Destiny of Disney Empire," *Los Angeles Times*, December 1, 1968.

10 "Disneyland Hails Its 100 Millionth," *Los Angeles Times*, June 18, 1971.

11 Karal Ann Marling, *Designing Disney's Theme Parks: the Architecture of Reassurance.* (Montreal: Centre canadien d'architecture, 1997), 14.

12 Barry Bearak, "Florida's EPCOT Center will Combine Two Theme Parks," *Los Angeles Times*, August 27, 1982.

13 "Disneyland to Overhaul 'Fantasy' Area of Park," *Los Angeles Times*, January 18, 1982.

14 Dorene Koehler, *The Mouse and the Myth: Sacred Art and Secular Ritual at Disneyland* (Indiana University, 2017), 140.

15 Diana Griego, "Disneyland Opens Revamped 'Alice'," *Los Angeles Times*, April 14, 1984.

16 John Hench and Peggy Van Pelt, *Designing Disney: Imagineering and the Art of the Show* (New York: Disney Editions, 2003), 13.

17 Kimi Yoshino, "Disney Brings Submarine Ride Back From the Depths," *Los Angeles Times*, June 11, 2007.

18 Richard Verrier and Dave McKibben, "Disney to Fix a Major Misstep; California Adventure, A Disappointment its Opening, Will Receive a $1.1-Billion Overhaul," *Los Angeles Times*, October 17, 2007.

19 Beth Dunlop, *Building A Dream: The Art of Disney Architecture* (New York: Abrams, 1996), 26.

Additional Citations

p. 263 "Almost all artworks…": *The Ceramic Mural: Modern Use of An Ancient Art*, filmed by Norman Wright Productions, Walt Disney Productions, 1967.

p. 271 "It took eleven years…": John Hench and Peggy Van Pelt, *Designing Disney: Imagineering and the Art of the Show* (New York: Disney Editions, 2003), 12.

p. 277 "The idea was…": Ed Gross, "Creating Star Wars: George Lucas in His Own Words," *Empire*, April 14, 2017, https://www.empireonline.com/movies/features/creating-star-wars-george-lucas-words/.

p. 299 Reference to Marc Davis, Walt Disney, and Country Bear Jamboree: *The Imagineers, Walt Disney Imagineering: A Behind the Dreams Look at Making the Magic Real* (New York: Hyperion, 1996).

p. 317 "Virtual Reality is basically nothing new…": *The Imagineers, Walt Disney Imagineering: A Behind the Dreams Look at Making the Magic Real* (New York: Hyperion, 1996), 91.

Selected Bibliography

Barrett, Katherine, and Richard Greene. *Inside the Dream: The Personal Story of Walt Disney*. New York: Disney Editions, 2001.

Bright, Randy. *Disneyland: Inside Story*. New York: Abrams, 1987.

Broggie, Michael. *Walt Disney's Railroad Story: The Small-Scale Fascination That Led to a Full-Scale Kingdom*. Pasadena, CA: Pentrex Media Group, 1998.

Childs, Valerie. *The Magic of Disneyland and Walt Disney World*. New York: Mayflower Books, 1979.

Cline, Rebecca, and Steven Clark. *The Walt Disney Studios: A Lot to Remember*. Glendale, CA: Disney Editions, 2016.

Comras, Kelly. *Ruth Shellhorn*. Athens, GA: The University of Georgia Press, 2016.

Crump, Rolly. *It's Kind of a Cute Story*. Baltimore, MD: Bamboo Forest Publishing, 2012.

Dunlop, Beth. *Building a Dream: The Art of Disney Architecture*. New York: Abrams, 1996.

Emerton, Bruce, and Chris Nichols. *Built by Becket*. Los Angeles: Los Angeles Conservancy Modern Committee, 2003.

Finch, Christopher. *The Art of Walt Disney: From Mickey Mouse to the Magic Kingdoms*. New York: Abrams, 2011.

Gabler, Neal. *Walt Disney: The Triumph of the American Imagination*. New York: Knopf, 2007.

Gennaway, Sam. *The Disneyland Story: The Unofficial Guide to the Evolution of Walt Disney's Dream*. Birmingham, AL: Keen Communications, 2013.

Gennaway, Sam. *Walt and the Promise of Progress City*. Pike Road, AL: Ayefour, 2011.

Gordon, Bruce, David Mumford, Roger Le Roque, and Nick Farago. *Disneyland the Nickel Tour: A Postcard Journey Through a Half Century of the Happiest Place on Earth*. Santa Clarita, CA: Camphor Tree, 2000.

Gordon, Bruce, and Tim O'Day. *Disneyland: Then, Now, and Forever*. New York: Disney Editions, 2006.

Gurr, Bob. Design: *Just For Fun*. Riverside, CA: Ape Pen Publishing & Gurr Designs, 2012.

Hahn, Don. *Yesterday's Tomorrow: Disney's Magical Mid-Century*. Glendale: Disney Editions, 2017.

Handke, Daniel, Vanessa Hunt, and Tony Baxter. *Poster Art of Disney Parks*. New York: Disney Editions, 2012.

Hench, John, and Peggy Van Pelt. *Designing Disney: Imagineering and the Art of the Show*. New York: Disney Editions, 2003.

Hess, Alan. *Googie Redux: Ultramodern Roadside Architecture*. San Francisco: Chronicle Books, 2004.

Hunt, William Dudley. *Total Design: Architecture of Welton Becket and Associates*. New York: McGraw-Hill, 1972.

Jacobs, David. *Disney's America on Parade: A History of the U.S.A. in a Dazzling, Fun-Filled Pageant*. New York: H. N. Abrams, 1975.

Kothenschulte, Daniel, ed. *The Walt Disney Film Archives. The Animated Movies 1921–1968*. Cologne: TASCHEN, 2016.

Kurtti, Jeff. *Walt Disney's Imagineering Legends and the Genesis of the Disney Theme Park*. New York: Disney Publishing, 2008.

Kurtti, Jeff, and Bruce Gordon. *The Art of Disneyland*. Glendale: Disney Editions, 2005.

Marling, Karal Ann, and Donna R. Braden. *Behind the Magic: 50 Years of Disneyland*. Dearborn, MI: The Henry Ford, 2005.

Marling, Karal Ann. *Designing Disney's Theme Parks: The Architecture of Reassurance*. Montreal: Centre canadien d'architecture, 1997.

Mattie, Erik. *World's Fairs*. New York: Princeton Architectural Press, 1998.

Moore, Charles, Peter Becker, and Regula Campbell. *The City Observed, Los Angeles: A Guide to Its Architecture and Landscapes*. New York: Vintage Books, 1984.

Mumford, David, and Bruce Gordon, ed. *A Brush with Disney: An Artist's Journey, Told Through the Words and Works of Herbert Dickens Ryman*. Santa Clarita, CA: Camphor Tree, 2000.

Newcomb, Horace. *Encyclopedia of Television*. New York: Fitzroy Dearborn, 2004.

Pierce, Todd James. *Three Years in Wonderland: The Disney Brothers, C. V. Wood, and the Making of the Great American Theme Park*. Jackson, MS: University Press of Mississippi, 2016.

Price, Harrison. *Walt's Revolution!: By the Numbers*. Orlando, FL: Ripley Entertainment, 2004.

Reynolds, Robert R. *Roller Coasters, Flumes & Flying Saucers: The Story of Ed Morgan & Karl Bacon, Ride Inventors of the Modern Amusement Parks*. Jupiter, FL: Northern Lights Pub, 1999.

Sklar, Marty, Ray Bradbury, and Richard M. Sherman. *Dream It! Do It!: My Half-Century Creating Disney's Magic Kingdoms*. New York: Disney Editions, 2013.

Smith, Dave. *Disney A to Z: The Official Encyclopedia*. New York: Hyperion, 1996.

Solomon, Charles. *The Disney That Never Was: The Stories and Art from Five Decades of Unproduced Animation*. New York: Hyperion, 1995.

Smith, Dave. *The Quotable Walt Disney*. New York: Disney Editions, 2001.

Stanton, Jeffrey. *Venice California: Coney Island of the Pacific*. Los Angeles: Donahue, 1993.

Stephens, E. J., and Marc Wanamaker. *Griffith Park*. Charleston, SC: Arcadia, 2011.

Surrell, Jason. *The Disney Mountains: Imagineering at Its Peak*. New York: Disney Editions, 2007.

Surrell, Jason. *The Haunted Mansion: From the Magic Kingdom to the Movies*. New York: Welcome Enterprises, 2009.

Surrell, Jason. *Pirates of the Caribbean: From the Magic Kingdom to the Movies*. New York: Disney Editions, 2007.

Thomas, Bob. *Walt Disney: An American Original*. Glendale: Disney Editions, 2012.

Walt Disney Productions. *Disneyland: The First Thirty Years*. Walt Disney Productions, 1985.

Acknowledgments

Walt Disney has become an almost mythic figure, so I am especially grateful to have the voices of those who knew and worked with him: Disney legends Rolly Crump, Richard M. Sherman, Marty Sklar, and especially Bob Gurr. My wife, Charlene Nichols, brought her love of engineering and science to the story while creating order from our mountain of research materials; all historians wish they were married to a librarian.

This project would not have come to life without Lawrence Schiller, Benedikt Taschen, and my editor Nina Wiener, who kept the trains running through all kinds of weather. Anna-Tina Kessler made it look great. Also with TASCHEN, Erica Pak, Pimploy Phongsirivech, Stefan Klatte, Maurene Appelhans, Sarah Wrigley, Frances Molina, and Martin Holz deserve appreciation.

I have never worked with a more enthusiastic and brilliant team of archivists than Rebecca Cline and Kevin M. Kern at the Walt Disney Archives, Disney photo researchers Holly Brobst and Michael Buckhoff, and Walt Disney Imagineering's Vanessa Hunt and David Stern. Thanks to Daniel Saeva, Angela M. Ontiveros, Ashley W. Leonard, Stephanie L. Everett, and Shiho Tilley at Disney Publishing for working behind the scenes to keep the project on track. I also want to acknowledge the contributions of Disney's Larry Berger, Max Calne, Jeff Fischer, Jacob Genzuk, Jennifer Liu, Betsy Mercer, Beatrice Osman, Bill Scollon, Dave Smith, and Wendy Thompson.

I appreciate the research and writing of Braden Graeber; writing and copyediting of Teena Apeles; fact-checking assistance and encouragement from Greg Abbott, Kiara Geller, Michael Giaimo, Kevin Kidney, Leonard Maltin, Chris Merritt, Tim O'Day, Jordan Reichek, and Mark Walsh; and proofreading by Anna Skinner. Adriene Biondo, Alison Brantley, William Choi, Rachel Elizabeth, Freddy Mulbarger, and Dkutla Osterhagen were great researchers, as were the keepers of more than 70 collections we examined: especially Eli Attie, John T. Ball (University of Akron); Claudia Bianchi (Laif); Bob Blankman (First American Corp.); Michelle Butnick-Press and Joelle Sedlmeyer (Getty Images); Karen Carpenter (John G. Zimmerman Archive); William D. Caughlin and Sheldon Hochheiser, Ph.D. (AT&T); Linda Cervon, Heather David, and Dave DeCaro (Daveland); Simon Elliott (University of California, Los Angeles); Leigh Gleason (University of California, Riverside/California Museum of Photography); Jan Grenci and Alexis Valentine (Library of Congress); Karin Hellmann (dpa); Susan Hodgson (Gordon R. Howard Museum); Andy Howick (mptv); Chris Hunter (General Electric); David Kuntz; Roxann Livingston; Jennifer McFadden (*National Geographic*); Caitlin Moneypenny-Johnston (Walt Disney Family Museum); Jane Newell (Anaheim Public Library); Nathaniel Parks (Art Institute of Chicago); Bob Roberts, Faye Thompson, and Matthew Severson (Academy of Motion Picture Arts and Sciences); Bernie Shine, David Starkman, Thomas Struth, Tim Street-Porter, and Dace Taube (University of Southern California); Erica Varela (*Los Angeles Times*); Marc Wanamaker (Bison Archives); Antoinette Watson, Jennifer Watts, and Stephanie Arias (Huntington Library, Art Museum, and Botanical Gardens); Miranda Rectenwald (Washington University in St. Louis); Colleen Haggerty (Bank of America); Stephen Hall (University of Arizona); and Shaun Kirkpatrick (Chubb).

A final round of thanks goes out to Kent Bulza, Joe Campana, Rachel Gould, Alex Evans, Alan Hess, Lisa Hernandez, Milt Larsen, Jack Laxer, Raymond Persi, Charles Phoenix, Jeptha Storm, and Jeremy Winkworth; Robert E. Van Oosting and LeRoy Schmaltz; Matt Segal and my colleagues at *Los Angeles* magazine; and to my mom, Cheryl Pease, who loved Disneyland as much as I do.

—*Chris Nichols, 2018*

ENDPAPERS **A 1958 fun map of Disneyland featuring attractions to come. *Art, Sam McKim***

PAGES 2-3 **Walt Disney described his park on television in 1954.**

FOLDOUT **An early concept for Disneyland's entrance.**

PAGE 8 **Three ways to explore Fantasyland in 1970: by boat, rail, or lift. *Photo, Dean Conger***

PAGES 10-11 **The original Disneyland sign on Harbor Boulevard welcomed guests from 1958 to 1989. Its bold colors, shapes, and kinetic exuberance make it an icon of midcentury design.**

OPPOSITE **Pluto and his admirers, 1964. *Photo, Lawrence Schiller***

All images in this volume are copyright © Disney Enterprises, Inc., unless otherwise noted. Any omissions for copyright or credit are unintentional, and appropriate credit will be given in future editions if such copyright holders contact the publisher. Courtesy Disney: 21, 38 above, 51, 71, 76 above, 108 above, 110–111, 138, 176, 179 above, 198, 224, 225, 245 below.

Text by Chris Nichols. Additional captions Braden Graeber and Teena Apeles. The opinions expressed by this book's authors do not necessarily represent the views of The Walt Disney Company. The following are some of the trademarks and service marks owned by Disney Enterprises, Inc. or its affiliates: Adventureland; *Audio-Animatronics*; Disney; Disneyland Park; Disneyland Resort; Fantasyland; Frontierland; Imagineering; Imagineers; Magic Kingdom; Main Street, U.S.A.; Splash Mountain; Tomorrowland; Walt Disney World; Pixar.

Many of the images included in this volume were obtained from Disney's own treasure troves. Special thanks to Walt Disney Imagineering, Walt Disney Archives and Photo Library, and the Disney Library Restoration and Preservation teams, who provided valuable research materials and expertise.

Image Credits
Courtesy Greg Abbott: 50 below. Courtesy Anaheim Public Library [Accession #P8897]: 80–81. Courtesy of AT&T Archives and History Center: 201, 254. David Attie: 162, 192. From the collection of Heather M. David: 25 above, 117. Collection of Dave DeCaro, davelandweb.com: 10–11, 65 below, 70 above, 72, 77, 112, 114–115, 121 above, 139 above, 170–171, 202, 236, 237 above, 268 above. Courtesy Everett Collection: 134, 270. From the Collections of The Henry Ford Museum. Gift of Ford Motor Company: 26. GE and the GE Monogram are trademarks of General Electric Company and are used with permission: 217. General Electric Archives, miSci, Museum of Innovation & Science: 219 below. © Getty Images: Ib Andersen/Found Image Holdings/Corbis, 29 above; Archive Photos, 46; Bettmann, 22, 34, 147 below, 151 below, 161 below, 164–165, 189; Ralph Crane/The LIFE Picture Collection, 118, 120–121, 137, 145, 146, 199 below, 200, 206 below, 209, 248–249; Loomis Dean/The LIFE Picture Collection, 67, 73 below, 78, 129, 155, 167, 168, 196, 197, 203; Alfred Eisenstaedt/Time Life Pictures, 41, 44; Allan Grant/The LIFE Picture Collection, 128, 130–131, 132; Hulton Archive, 223 above; Earl Leaf/Michael Ochs Archives, 73 above; Gene Lester/Archive Photos, 31; David McNew/Hulton Archive/Newsmakers, 316; Jorge Villalba, 317. © J. Paul Getty Trust. Getty Research Institute, Los Angeles (2004.R.10): 52–53. Courtesy of Bob Gurr: 194 below. Courtesy Jim Heimann Collection: 29 below. Courtesy Kevin Kidney: 186. Photographed by George S. Kuntz, MD, digitally restored by David W. Kuntz: 122, 126–127. Bertrand Laforet/Gamma/laif: 74 below. Lawry's Restaurants, Inc.: 28. LOOK Magazine Photograph Collection, Library of Congress, Prints & Photographs Division: LC-L9-59-4408-FF, fr 12, 79; LC-L901A-56-4175, fr 55, 47; © Earl Theisen Archives, LC-L9-54-1567-A, fr 34, 38 below, LC-L9-60-8812, frame 8, 18. Los Angeles Public Library: Herald/Examiner Collection, 56, 74 above, 140 above, 144 below, 150. Los Angeles Times Photographic Archives, Library Special Collections, Charles E. Young Research Library, UCLA: 647460 (Collection 1808), 113; 4233338 (Collection 1429), 245 above. © MPTV/mptvimages.com: Bernie Abramson, 195 above; Sid Avery, 66, 169; Leo Fuchs, 148–149. National Geographic Creative: Dean Conger, 8; Thomas Nebbia, 15, 62, 68–69, 75, 82, 87, 88–89, 174–175, 210–211, 221. © Picture Alliance/AP Images: 54–55;

Edward Kitch, 109; Ellis Bosworth, 183. Courtesy Jordan Reichek: 97 above, 139 below, 179 below. © Lawrence Schiller, Polaris Communications Inc., Rights Reserved: 12, 76 below, 92–93, 101, 102–103, 156, 157, 193 below, 208, 212–213, 327. Schneider-Cash © AGE Fotostock: 265. © Willard Smith/Planet Pix via ZUMA Wire: 36 above. © Tim Street–Porter: 294–295. © Thomas Struth: 278–279, 314–315. TAM Collection: 25 below, 50 above, 63. © Earl Theisen Archives: 18, 27, 38 below. Marc Tulane/Gamma/laif: 292. Courtesy of University of Southern California, on behalf of the USC Libraries Special Collections: 160, 166. Walt Disney with daughters Diane and Sharon, c. 1942; silver gelatin photograph; collection of the Walt Disney Family Foundation: 27. © Marc Wanamaker/Bison Archives: 30, 135 above. Photo by Delmar Watson/Watson Family Photo Archive: 58. Courtesy John G. Zimmerman Archive: 250. © John G. Zimmerman Archive: 223 below.

Trademark Notices
Academy Award® and Academy of Motion Picture Arts and Sciences® are registered trademarks of the Academy of Motion Picture Arts and Sciences. Bank of America® is a registered trademark of the Bank of America Corporation. GE® is a trademark of General Electric Company. RICHFIELD Oil is the registered trademark owned by Andeavor and its affiliate companies and is used with permission. Technicolor® is a registered trademark of Technicolor, Inc. Upjohn Pharmaceuticals is the registered trademark owned by Pfizer Inc. and its affiliate companies and is used with permission.

EACH AND EVERY TASCHEN BOOK PLANTS A SEED!
TASCHEN is a carbon neutral publisher. Each year, we offset our annual carbon emissions with carbon credits at the Instituto Terra, a reforestation program in Minas Gerais, Brazil, founded by Lélia and Sebastião Salgado. To find out more about this ecological partnership, please check: www.taschen.com/zerocarbon
Inspiration: unlimited. Carbon footprint: zero.

To stay informed about TASCHEN and our upcoming titles, please subscribe to our free magazine at www.taschen.com/magazine, follow us on Instagram and Facebook, or e-mail your questions to contact@taschen.com.

Concept, composition, and design by TASCHEN GmbH

TASCHEN GmbH
Hohenzollernring 53, D-50672 Köln
www.taschen.com

Editor Nina Wiener, New York
Art direction and design Anna-Tina Kessler, Los Angeles

Printed in China
ISBN 978-3-8365-6348-2